I0170077

GOD, AM I
DATING
THE RIGHT PERSON?

Receiving The Warning Signs That We Sometimes
Miss

DANIELLE WILIAMS

Self-Published by Danielle Williams

Copyright © 2017 by Danielle Williams

All rights reserved. No part of this book may be reproduced in any form or by any means without the prior written consent of the Publisher, except in the use of brief quotes used in reviews.

All scriptures are taken from King James Version (KJV) of the Bible unless otherwise denoted.

Scriptures noted KJV are from the Holy Bible: KING JAMES VERSION Copyright 1982 by Thomas Nelson, Inc. Used by permission. All rights reserved.

ISBN: 978-0-9977141-1-1

Contents

PREFACE

This book was written to help other single Christians, like myself, understand who they are in Christ and allow them the ability to avoid the pitfalls Satan has set for believers in the realm of dating. I married at a very early age; therefore, I missed the single experience. At one time in my life, I believed all it took for a marriage to work was love and things in common. However, after my divorce, I was thrust back into the dating arena, which I initially tried to avoid, by marrying the man I thought was the one.

In this book, you will find keys to becoming the holy, saved believer God has called you to be. You will also learn characteristics that you should possess and that you should expect and require of those who romantically peek your interest. Today is the day we begin to make wise decisions about our lives and expect the same of those who are in constant communication with us.

My inspiration for writing this book is empowering other believers to walk the narrow path God has for us, realizing that the path that leads to destruction is wide, and along that broad path, anything goes. For instance, on the broad path, we can date non-believers; we can live with our boyfriends; we can date as many people at one time as we desire and not feel bad or convicted about it in spite of the fact that we are not married. On the narrow path that leads to life, we have to follow commandments, standards, morals, and instructions. We must always remember that we are ambassadors of Christ, and He has a good plan for our lives.

INTRODUCTION
Never Allow a Relationship to Keep You From Obeying God's Word.

In Genesis 2:18, 21-23, it says, "The Lord God said, 'It is not good that the man should be alone; I will make a help-meet for him.' And the Lord God caused a deep sleep to fall upon Adam, and he slept: and he took one of his ribs, and closed up the flesh instead thereof; And the rib, which the Lord God had taken from man, made he a woman, and brought her unto the man. And Adam said, 'This is now bone of my bones, and flesh of my flesh: she shall be called Woman because she was taken out of man.'"

From the beginning of time, God ordained that the woman was made for the man. The man was alone in the Garden minding his own business before God made a woman for him. Why do we think things have changed today? The Bible says that Jesus Christ is the same yesterday, today, and forever (Hebrews 13:8). We as single Christians must take our place in the will of God. Adam had a wonderful relationship with God before the woman was made for him. He was in fellowship with God and walking in his purpose. Single men are to model this behavior, and single women are to be of like spirit with God.

What we are not to model is Adam and Eve's

3

disobedience to God. Adam did what many singles do in their walk with God; he got distracted once he was involved in his relationship with Eve. He had a wonderland in the Garden of Eden; he walked with God and talked to God each and every day. He heard the words and commands of God without error before Eve came along. Once Eve stepped on the scene, it appears Adam neglected the friendship and fellowship he had with God. In Genesis 2:15-17, it states, *"And the Lord God took the man, and put him into the Garden of Eden to dress it and to keep it. And the Lord God commanded the man, saying, 'Of every tree of the garden thou mayest freely eat: But of the tree of the knowledge of good and evil, thou shalt not eat of it: for in the day that thou eatest thereof thou shalt surely die.'"*

Genesis 3 tells the story of how the serpent deceived Eve — The serpent was more subtle than any beast of the field which the Lord God had made. And he said unto the woman, "Yea, hath God said, Ye shall not eat of every tree of the garden?" And the woman said, "We may eat of the fruit of the trees of the garden: but of the fruit of the tree which Is in the midst of the garden, God hath said, Ye shall not eat of it, neither shall ye touch it, lest ye die." And the serpent said unto the woman, "Ye shall not surely die: For God doth know that in the day ye eat thereof, then your eyes shall be opened, and ye shall be as gods, knowing good and evil." And when the woman saw that the tree was good for food and that it was pleasant to the eyes, and a tree to be desired to make one wise, she took of the fruit thereof, and did eat, and also gave unto her husband with her, and he did eat. And the eyes of them both were opened, and they knew that they were naked, and they sewed fig-leaves together, and made themselves aprons and hid from God.

Why did Adam and Eve not obey the Word of God? Why did they believe the lie of the serpent? The answer is simply that Adam was distracted by Eve. God had given Adam very specific orders, but when the temptation came, he totally disregarded those orders. In 1 Timothy 2:11-14 (NIV), it states, *"A woman should learn in quietness and full submission. I do not permit a woman to teach or to assume authority over a man she must be quiet. For Adam was formed first, then Eve. And Adam was not the one deceived; it was the woman who was deceived and became a sinner."*

After Adam had been married to Eve, he lost the connection and fellowship he once had with God. When we fellowship with God, it must be a continual, daily activity. You cannot fellowship with God once a month; because if you do, you give way to the serpent, which is always looking for a way to deceive you. By losing fellowship with God, Adam allowed Eve to persuade him to go against the plan of God. He began to esteem her desires above what God required of him. He chose to go along with Eve's program rather than God's.

In this book, I believe you will learn keys to staying in close fellowship and relationship with God. You will be able to identify the plots and schemes that the enemy sends your way to take you out of the will of God. It was just one act of disobedience that caused God to drive Adam out of the Garden and out of direct fellowship with Him. Adam had a choice to eat of every tree in the Garden except the tree of the knowledge of good and evil, but he couldn't resist. We believers should learn from Adam's mistake and have our personal relationship with God so strong that when tempted to disobey God and go against His Word, we will not do it and will stand strong on the Word of God. We do not want to neglect God or our God-given destiny. It is extremely important that we take the commands of God seriously and believe that what God says is so. If He says do not eat of the tree or you will die, we must definitively believe Him.

CHAPTER 1
LOVE

Jesus has a lot to teach us about love. Matthew 22:36-40 NIV states, "'Teacher, which is the greatest commandment in the Law?' Jesus replied: 'Love the Lord your God with all your heart and with all your soul and with all your mind. This is the first and greatest commandment. And the second is like it: Love your neighbor as yourself. All the Law and the Prophets hang on these two commandments.'" Once we get to a certain age, we begin to desire love and affection from the opposite sex. Depending on our childhood and the relationship we experienced with our parents, as well as their relationship towards each other, these experiences may affect our love lives in either a positive or negative manner.

I grew up with my mother and father in the same household. My parents were the biggest influence in my relationships as an adult. They were not saved; and therefore, everything was out of balance. My dad was married, but separated from his wife and involved in a relationship with my mother when I was conceived. He had numerous extramarital relationships, and my mom drowned herself in work to avoid his behavior. This affected me tremendously. I cried so many times for what my dad was doing to us. My father allowed my mother to lead the household, while he lived a selfish lifestyle which was pleasing to him.

As a child growing up, I had gone to church no more than 20 times. We did not attend Sunday school or Bible studies; we went on Sundays, and I randomly visited church with family members and friends. I had no real connection with God. What I knew about love and life, I learned from my surroundings.

Most people were not raised in happy, loving, godly homes. For many of us, our parents seemed happy maybe 20% of the time. Majorly busy with work and providing for us, they spent very little time nurturing their marriages and relationships. For us children, we began to desire love, hugs, kisses, and companionship from the opposite sex by at least age 12. Despite how bad our home lives were, it's a natural desire that burns within us.

In the Bible, we can find many examples of

how falling in love can go wrong. In 2 Samuel 13, Tamar was raped by her half-brother; when her dad, King David, heard of it, he was angry but took no action in protecting her or disciplining his son. In Genesis 20, we find the story of Abraham who told King Abimelech that Sarah was his sister because he was afraid he would kill him for her. God had to visit the king in a dream to tell him not to touch her lest he dies. But the King was innocent and was lied to by the both of them.

Some of us have stories of how love has failed us. We have been disappointed by our parents, personal relationships, and marriages, which ended on bad terms; and subsequently, some of us need help coping with the disappointment as well as with our next move in God. We often know from the beginning of the relationship that it may not be the best choice, but we go along for the ride anyway, hoping that God will bless our relationship, only to find ourselves back at the drawing board questioning God about His will for us and why we cannot find "the one."

It is so vital to have that one-on-one personal relationship with Him, where we hear and know His voice before we start dating. If you have not found yourself in God first, you will endure a lot of heartache and pain. Finding God before dating means you know your purpose in life, you know why God has created you, and you know that women are ordained to submit to their husbands who are their leaders—not their bosses anyway. If you have dated first or gotten married first and then found God, there is hope for you. It is not the end of the world. God wishes that none of us perish but that all should come to repentance (2 Peter 3:9).

I, myself, knew of God but did not have that true, personal and intimate relationship with Him before dating. At the age of 17 going on 18, I left home to join the U.S. Navy. This was my first separation from home, friends, and family, and it was exactly what God had ordained for me. I found God and my prayer life began when I went to the military. I saw the world for the first time through my own eyes, and it was scary. I began to be hit on by married men and witness all types of sexual sin. It was a very eye-opening experience.

MY RELATIONSHIP WITH GOD

As I recollect, I believe my relationship with God began in boot camp. Boot camp was where I began to have challenges in life and that brought forth my need for God. I began to pray, go to Sunday services, read the Word and search for God on my own, which gave me peace to make it through that process. Once boot camp was over, I headed to Japan for my duty station, the place in which I would spend the next 4 years of my career.

When I made it to Japan, I found a church on base and began to frequent those services. I could not have been happier; I had new friends, new sites, shopping, and stories to tell all my family and friends at home. This is also where I met the man I would date for the next 3 years and soon marry. He had become my "home away from home." We were best friends and did everything together, and I loved him dearly. He would become one of the biggest regrets of my life and eventually a great learning opportunity for me.

LOVE AND MARRIAGE

When I first met my husband-to-be, we were working together, and it was love at first sight. He was everything I wanted physically in a man: TALL, DARK, & HANDSOME. He had a beautiful smile, smooth skin, was very athletic and extremely cool; everyone loved him. When we met, he was not dating anyone, and I actually approached him as a friend. I found out that we both liked rap music, which, at 18 years old, I figured that was something we had in common.

We had "a ball" together; we were inseparable; his friends were my friends, and my friends were his friends.

We traveled the world together and did many new things together: we rode elephants, jet-skied, and journeyed through different places, sightseeing places such as Australia. We loved it and loved each other. We also traveled home and met each other's families. I met his parents and siblings, and they were all very nice people. He came home with me and met my family; everyone loved him. Together, we established tangible goals to be accomplished after we both separated from the military. We saved all of our money together and budgeted our paychecks by giving ourselves an allowance through the week and splurged on the weekends. When we traveled home on our vacations, we did a lot of shopping and spent a lot of money just enjoying life.

The entire 3 years I dated this man, he was a complete gentleman. I got saved, and we were in church all the time. One year, for Valentine's Day, he gave me a Bible as a gift; this made me so happy. While we dated, we told each other everything that was going on in our lives; we were best friends. If a girl tried to talk to him behind my back, he told me. If one of his male friends wanted him to go out and do something that would hurt our relationship, he ran it past me first. When he had to work and could not leave the ship, I would go out, get his dinner and bring it back to him and vice versa; we were inseparable.

We were in love and conversed about getting married and pictured our lives together outside the military. We had only been dating a short period and getting married would have meant that I would have been transferred to a different command, resulting in a long distance relationship for us; so, we extended our engagement and waited for marriage to avoid those ramifications. Subsequently, I began to get convicted when we had sex, so we became celibate until our wedding date. Our love just grew and grew, and we were getting closer and closer, and I could not be happier.

When my enlistment ended, I left Japan and came back home and started to get things together for the wedding. While we were separated, I missed him and was having a lot of doubts about marrying him. We talked often, and he declared his love for me and assured me he loved me and would never do anything to hurt me. We put a lot of money into this wedding and had family and friends coming from all over, so we had to go forward with it. I could never disappoint him as well as everyone I loved by backing out of the wedding.

We did it! I got all dressed up and went to the church. As I was reluctantly walking down that aisle, I knew I was making a huge mistake. Even after the wedding, while we were on our honeymoon, I felt that the veil was lifted from my eyes and it was clear that I had made the wrong decision; but, what could I do now? I loved him. I truly did, but I wrestled in my mind and had to shake off this nagging feeling that I had made a mistake.

MARRIED LIFE

Once we were married and settled in our new home, it became very clear that we were like night and day. He began to get new friends at his new command that he wanted to go to lunch with and hang out with on the weekends and I was just left at home like an old housewife. We still did things together, like go out of town, go to water parks, to the movies, visit shopping outlets and our families, but there was a great distance between us. I would ask him over and over again if he was happy, he always said yes that he was happy and assured me that everything was okay. So, I dealt with it. I did what was becoming natural to me, I prayed as he did what came natural to him, went out.

While we were married, my husband was very sneaky and did a lot of things behind my back. I was in school full time making the grade, while he was out hanging in the streets. I trusted him with my life, so the thought of him being unfaithful never crossed my mind. I thought our love would sustain us. I thought the years we were together and the promises we made to each other meant something. All the trust I had in him allowed him the freedom and opportunity to hang himself.

In our marriage, things began to unfold and God began to reveal my husband's actions to me in dreams and through a girlfriend of mine. One of my friends had a picture of my husband and me in her home. One day, while my friend's neighbor was visiting for a few moments, the neighbor saw my husband in the picture and said, "Who is that with him? He's talking to my girl." My friend really did not want to share this information with me because she knew it would hurt me, but when she did, I was truly thankful.

It was as if I knew something was going on in my heart. I confronted him, and he denied it. Not only did he deny it, but he got totally out of character with my friend, while talking to her and called her out her name. That is how I knew he was guilty. I spoke to the girl; she was honest and let me know it was true that my husband was trying to date her. I placed this incident "on the shelf."

There was a weekend he had traveled to another state and turned his cell phone off the

entire weekend. I called and called and called
and had no way to get in touch with him the
entire weekend. When he returned home, he
assured me everything was okay, but somehow I
was able to check the voicemail on his phone and
heard a young lady's voice wishing him a safe
journey back home, calling him "Bae," and letting
him know she had a lovely weekend. I called her,
but she denied everything. She too was married,
and I found that out at the end of my marriage.
My husband denied anything happened. I cried
and cried and cried, but I was in denial and loved
him so much that I believed his lie.

As time went on, this woman and that
weekend never left my heart and mind. I asked
him repeatedly, "Did anything happen that
weekend?" He had to tell me NO 1,000 times and
even called me crazy. I felt alone and very
lonely. Our personal time became no time at all.
He never called to talk to me or check on me
while he was at work away from home. He
became consumed with work, which I later found
out that was the excuse he used to be able to
talk to his other women.

So, since I was now a child of God, who had
learned how to fast and pray, I began to do just
that, and the Lord began to reveal things to me.
One night my husband called me and asked if I
wanted him to bring me anything home to eat.
He had a break and was going to come run home
for a minute. I said yes and asked him to bring

me a burger from McDonald's. We had a prepaid phone; so apparently while my husband was on his way home, he used that phone to call that same woman from his weekend getaway. I was clueless that night. So, he came home, brought me the food and went back to work; that was a Saturday night. Subsequently, the next morning was a Sunday; I got up and got dressed, and the Holy Spirit told me to check the call log on the prepaid phone, and I did. To my surprise, I saw the same phone number that I had called months prior and spoke to the woman that denied anything happened between the two of them. This was it!

That morning, I went on to church and left him asleep in bed, which was totally abnormal for us. I went home and acted like nothing had happened. I began to make a plan for myself. I planned to leave him and within a week, I did. We talked; I asked him to admit what was going on with the young lady he was with that weekend, but he refused. I was extremely hurt, yet knew in my spirit he was lying to me. I left him. After this, more dirt surfaced in regards to what he was doing; it all came out. He let me leave, and he continued living his life as a bachelor as if I never existed. This went on for a few months.

We filed for divorce. I was hurt but knew without a doubt that I could not be with a man who had been so unfaithful to me. He tried to

17

stop the divorce, went to the courthouse, and told the divorce mediation representative we were going to work it out. When I heard this, I had him go right back down there and turn those papers back into the court. The last thing I wanted in the world was an adulterous fornicator who had no respect for God or me. I was a virgin when I met him; and since he could not respect me, I could not be with him.

AFTER THE DIVORCE

So we divorced, and as a result, I had to deal with a lot of pain. Because as a child, I witnessed the wrongful things my dad did to my mother, I could not forgive my husband. I was determined not to live with an unfaithful spouse. Because of the different women and all of the lies he told me, in which I had to go undercover to find out the truth, I could not do it anymore. I desired peace and love in marriage, not lies and deceit. I figured it was more painful to live with him than live without him.

It took a very long time for me to get over all the pain, lost love, and dreams. It would take even longer for me to trust men again. Even though I had doubts about getting married to him, I still loved him and truly thought because we simply loved each other, it would work. I never thought in a million years he would lie and cheat on me the way he did.

After we had wedded, I saw an entirely different side of him and began to learn that people are not all they pretend to be. Some people believe the cliché: "What you don't know won't hurt you." But in my opinion, withholding information in a relationship is not advantageous because the truth eventually comes out. We must seek wisdom from the Lord for clarity on who He has sent into our lives and who the enemy has sent.

I went through a season of depression. I was upset with my ex-husband and God. I cried and cried and cried and did not want my marriage to fail; neither did I want to feel like a failure. My desire was to get married to live right; I never knew or had a clue about all it took to have a successful, godly marriage.

CHAPTER 2
PREREQUISITES

Before we can ask God the question, "Am I dating the right person?" we must be in right standing with Him. God has some very direct standards for His people, and He expects our obedience to His word if we want to be in fellowship with Him. Psalm 66:16-18 NIV says, *"Come and hear, all you who fear God; let me tell you what he has done for me. I cried out to him with my mouth; his praise was on my tongue. If I had cherished sin in my heart, the Lord would not have listened."*

The word of God says if we cherish sin in our heart, He will not hear us. It is important for us to be aware of the fact that God sees and knows everything and that He desires us to live honest, clean lives before Him. When we come before God in prayer, we must first be clear of any sin. Cherishing sin means you enjoy this particular sin

21

you are committing and you are unwilling to let it go. Please, do not think that God will accept your excuses. If you are praying to God and in sin, He does not hear you; you are wasting your time. You must repent of your sin, and stop that act that is against God, to receive an answer from God.

There were some key ingredients missing in my life even though I was a child of God. I was not being led by God; I was not submitted to God; I did not have an intimate relationship with God; I did not know how to wait on God for an answer; I did not know how to examine a person's fruit; and I did not know the plan of God for my life. I was attending church before I got married, but I did not have a strong, intimate relationship with God.

In 1 Thessalonians 5:16-18 NIV, the Bible says to, *"Rejoice always, pray continually, give thanks in all circumstances; for this is God's will for you in Christ Jesus."* I was not praying without ceasing; I was not fasting for answers from God, and neither was I seeking God like I was supposed to do. My personal relationship with the Lord began after I got connected with the wrong man, which was totally backward.

Matthew 6:33 says to "seek first the kingdom of God and his righteousness, and all these things will be added unto you." The correct way to date is to seek God first, have an intimate relationship with Him, where you hear His voice, in which He can correct you as needed. If you do not have that type of relationship with God, where He speaks to you, corrects, and guides you please—I implore you—stop dating for a season. We must be in fellowship with God before we seek the face of a person in a relationship.

BE LED BY GOD

When dating, it is very important to be led by the Spirit of God. Having a real, personal, intimate relationship with the Lord is so important before you start to date. Being led by the Spirit of God will allow you to discern if this new person is from God or Satan. God will give you clues and signs if you are sensitive to the Spirit.

How are you to be led by God? You pray, fast, get away to your personal prayer closet and seek God's face until you receive your answer and instruction. You must know how God communicates with you. Do you hear Him, receive dreams, or see visions? You must sanctify yourself and make an effort to be 100% holy before God and make God your priority above anything else.

BE SUBMITTED TO GOD

According to www.oxforddictionaries.com © 2016 Oxford University Press, **submission** can be defined as the action or fact of accepting or yielding to a superior force or the will or authority of another person. Being submitted to God means you have died to your flesh and your desires and you are alive In Christ. The Bible says in Matthew 16:24, *"Then said Jesus unto his disciples, If any man will come after me, let him deny himself, and take up his cross, and follow me."* When you are submitted to God, His Word becomes one of the most important things in your life. When you are submitted to God, His presence becomes vital to you. When you are submitted to God, you put the things that please God first, so you begin to avoid fornication and ungodliness. You let rejection, bitterness, fear, low self-esteem, and disobedience go. Your flesh and your desire for a relationship come second to what God wants from you.

Submitting our dating lives to God may seem difficult to do at first because it is done in the unseen realm. We date by what we see and by who sees us. The approach the Lord wants us to take is trusting Him to see for us. We must be in tune with God when we date to avoid the pitfalls and traps that Satan has set for us.

FELLOWSHIP WITH GOD

Having true fellowship with the Lord requires right living. Revelation 3:20 says that *"Jesus stands at the door and knocks, if any man hears my voice, and open the door, I will come in to him and sup with him and he with me."* That is fellowship—communication with God; being in the presence of God. Create an atmosphere of praise and worship where the Spirit of God will feel welcomed. The Bible says as we draw near to God, He will draw near to us (James 4:8). The Lord desires an intimate, personal relationship with us, but we have work to do. We must live holy lives before God.

NO SEX OUTSIDE OF MARRIAGE

If you are fornicating, it will be very hard for you to see the real character of the person you are dating. Sex clouds your mind and perception. If you have sinned and had sex with him, but you desire to live right before God, repent and mean it. If you struggle with sex, you should fast, pray, and deny yourself until you see results. If you tell the person you are dating, sex outside of marriage is a sin, they may laugh at you. He may call you a hypocrite; he may decide to fast and abstain from sex with you depending on how "into you" he is. Do not let this distract you. If he fast and abstain with you, this does not mean they are your spouse; it just means they really want you. Pray harder.

My ex-husband abstained with me, fasted with me, and prayed with me, went to church with me, but did not have that personal relationship with God for himself. Do not be afraid to be honest with yourself about the person you are dating. Are they really saved? You can love him, but he may not be who God has for you. Just because a person says they have a relationship with God does not mean they do. Make sure you are hearing from God on this relationship.

There are several things you must do as a saved, single person to avoid fornication. First, avoid listening to R&B and RAP music. All of these songs either makes you want a relationship or sex. Secondly, you must avoid television shows that promote promiscuous lifestyles and ungodly character. Thirdly, unsaved friends that are having sex outside of marriage or shacking up must be cut off. I know this sounds strict and insane, but their worldly influences are affecting you. They are where the biggest seeds are sown in your life, you are linking arms with them in the spirit, and therefore, the lifestyle they are living will soon rub off on you. And finally, avoid previous sexual partners. People from your past are not your spouse, and you should not be acting as if they are. You are to submit your flesh to the Spirit of God. By recognizing that you were in sin, now you can say no to this ungodliness and mean it.

SELF-CONTROL

Psalm 119:9 says, "How can a young person stay on the path of purity? By living according to your Word." We, believers, come to a place in our Christian walk where we recognize the struggles in our life with living holy before God and abstaining from sex. We fall into temptation over and over again and hate ourselves for it. We begin to cry out to God for help and assistance with this. We say things like, God take the desire away. We sometimes even try to change the way we look or dress to stop attracting the opposite sex, but that will not work.

The Bible says to stay pure we must live according to the word of God. Psalm 119:11 says that we are to hide His word in our heart to keep ourselves from sinning against God. When we hide the word in our heart, it helps us in our time of temptation. We must begin to devote our lives and our minds to God to come out of perversion and sexual sin.

Self-control is a fruit of the Holy Spirit. If we want to have self-control, we should ask the Holy Spirit for it. Having self-control will allow you the strength to avoid ungodly atmospheres and people. Having self-control will give you strength over your flesh. You will beat your body as Paul says and place it under subjection to the power of God. You will not fall for every trap that Satan sends your way. You will have the strength to say, "I can do all things through Christ who strengthens me (Philippians 4:13). I have so much strength I am waiting until marriage for sex, Glory to God. I have so much strength I am walking away from this ungodly situation and seeking the face of God."

REPENT

According to www.oxforddictionaries.com © 2016 Oxford University Press, **repentance** can be defined as "the action of repenting; sincere regret or remorse." True repentance is stopping an action that displeases God and having a sincere desire to please Him more than your flesh. When you stop fornicating, what is the reason? Do not just stop sinning because you do not want to have a baby or catch a sexually transmitted disease. Stop sinning because you know it is not pleasing God. Our desire must be to please God. His Word says presenting our bodies as a living sacrifice is our reasonable service. It is the least and the best thing that we can do. To kick the habit of fornication, fast and abstain from all ungodly activities.

KNOW WHO YOU ARE IN GOD

Psalm 139:13-18

For you created my inmost being;

you knit me together in my mother's womb.

I praise you because I am fearfully and wonderfully made;

your works are wonderful; I know that full well.

My frame was not hidden from you

when I was made in the secret place,

when I was woven together in the depths of the earth.

Your eyes saw my unformed body;

all the days ordained for me were written in your book

before one of them came to be.

*How precious to me are your thoughts,*God!*

DANIELLE WILIAMS

How vast is the sum of them!

Were I to count them,
they would outnumber the grains of sand—
when I awake, I am still with you.

No one on earth knows you better than God—
not your mother, not your father, not even your
best friend. God knows us better than we know
ourselves. In the book of Jeremiah 1:5, the Bible
says, *"Before I formed you in the womb I knew
you before you were born I set you apart. I
appointed you as a prophet to the nations."* If
you ever have any questions about who you are,
why you are, or what you are, ask God. He is
Omniscient or all-knowing. He created the
heavens and the earth and knows everything
about you. No matter what type of upbringing
you had or what type of environment you may
have had to endure, God was there. He is
Omnipresent or everywhere at the same time.
God is with you and has been there from the
beginning of your life. He loves you, He knows
you, and He cares about you. He is waiting for us
to seek Him for direction and guidance into the
purpose and plan He has for our lives.

30

CHAPTER 3
READY TO DATE

Now that you are in right standing with God and are ready to start dating, there are a few things that you must be equipped with to be successful on the dating scene. It is vital to be submitted to God and to hear from God, but also, we all must have a spiritual covering and be surrounded with like-minded individuals who will support and offer counsel to us as needed. As we date more and more, it will be important for us to learn the difference between judging people and inspecting their fruit. God has a wealth of knowledge for us to be successful in our single life, which is found in submitting to His Word and His will for our life.

A SPIRITUAL COVERING

The Bible says "*if any man lacks wisdom, let him ask of God*" (James 1:5). I did not have the type of father who would intimidate the guy when I brought him home. My dad had no wisdom to shed in the area of dating. I assume it was because he was not saved and he was a ladies' man himself. My dad had several adulterous relationships while I was coming up. The first time I brought a boyfriend home to meet my dad, my dad shook his hand and welcomed him into our home, no questions asked. He would tell funny stories about me, but never inquired about the guy's intentions or plans in general.

For those of us that do not have our natural father in our lives or he is present but lacks wisdom and salvation, we must rely on the Holy Spirit and the Church as our spiritual covering. If your father is physically present but not over-protective or possessive of you because he is too busy living his life, it is essential that we make this connection to God. With the Holy Spirit, we have to be led. The Holy Spirit will not fight against our will. The Holy Spirit has the desired way for us to go. The Bible says in Matthew 7:13-14 that "*broad is the way that leads to destruction and many there be that goeth that way. Because straight is the gate and narrow is the way that leads to life and few there be that find it."*

Do not be the type of believer that feels it is unnecessary to talk and share your personal business and relationships with others. Keeping good counsel around you will be key to your success in dating, but please make sure the person giving you advice is godly. Make sure these counselors live their lives by the Word of God. Proverbs 11:14 says *"where no counsel is, the people fall, but in the multitude of counselors there is safety."*

The darkest times of my life came when I was not connected to a church home and was not receiving godly counsel. I experienced deep church hurt after my divorce. I was single and looking for godly leadership because I knew this was missing in my life. The woman of God I was following, built me up spiritually but also operated under a spirit of control. So when I began to grow into my calling, she rejected me and it really hurt me deeply. After this, I ran from one church to the next, never fully wanting to connect with another woman or leader in a church setting. This allowed the enemy to creep into my single life and it caused me to become stagnant in the things of God in a major way.

If you are connected to a church home, it will be important to have a relationship with the pastor of the church so he can instruct you on what is and is not appropriate. A pastor will be able to pray for you, give you guidance, and receive from God on your behalf. Staying connected to your church is very important. Hebrews 10:24-25 states, *"And let us consider one another to provoke unto love and to good works: Not forsaking the assembling of ourselves together, as the manner of some is; but exhorting one another: and so much the more, as ye see the day approaching."*

What you must do is work on getting your relationship with God on the right track. Go to worship service and Bible study on a consistent basis, this time of isolation can be a very lonely season of your life. The negative, un-purposeful things in your life must go. You are to fill the new gaps and spaces in your life with prayer, worship, praise, listening to & reading your Word—the Bible. This is a time of growth for you and God will move in a mighty way because He loves when we strive towards maturity in Him. The Bible says that God inhabits the praises of His people; we must desire to please God and live in expectation of His glory and favor.

BE A FRUIT INSPECTOR

In the book of Mark Chapter 11: 12-14, the Bible says, *"The next day as they were leaving*

Bethany, Jesus was hungry. Seeing in the distance a fig tree in leaf, he went to find out if it had any fruit. When he reached it, he found nothing but leaves, because it was not the season for figs. Then he said to the tree, 'May no one ever eat fruit from you again.' And his disciples heard him say it."

When Jesus saw the fig tree from a distance, he was excited as He thought He was about to get a treat; but instead, upon closer review, there was no fruit on it. How disappointing is it to meet a potential mate you find attractive, but upon getting to know them, you discover there is no real substance to them? We must take our time when meeting new people to engage them in conversation to see what they are all about.

HOW DO YOU EXAMINE FRUIT?

Being a fruit inspector means asking yourself questions like, is this person saved? Does he own a Bible? Does he have godly convictions and morals? Does he have a church home that they have visited within the last 30 days? Does he have a drug (popping pills or smoking weed) or alcohol problem? Is he a fornicator and does he use the "God knows my heart" phrase to validate him being a sinner?

If you answered yes to any of these, please

stop dating this man and seek Godly counsel. These are all the things you should be asking the person you are considering dating and praying about. Seek God; He will reveal the truth to you if you want it. Do not be desperate for love or a relationship; be desperate for a right relationship with God.

LIKE-MINDED BELIEVERS

Another very important key to maintaining your holiness is connecting to like-minded individuals. If you cannot find like-minded individuals but have a lot of friends, begin to push away from those friends who are bad influences on you. You know them, maybe those ones that promote promiscuity and worldliness. It is okay to have friends that are not on your level spiritually, as long as you are the leader and they are not encouraging you to do ungodly things. The Word of God says in Matthew 13:24-30 that He will separate the wheat from the tare. As long as those friends you have are not influencing you in a negative manner, stay connected. Remember you are called to be the light of the world (Matthew 5:14).

KNOW YOUR CALLING

In Romans 12:6-8 NIV, the Bible says *"we have different gifts, according to the grace given to each of us. If your gift is prophesying, then prophesy in accordance with your faith; if it is serving, then serve; if it is teaching, then teach; if it is to encourage, then give encouragement; if it is giving, then give generously; if it is to lead, do it diligently; if it is to show mercy, do it cheerfully."* It is very important that we know our purpose in God before we start dating. Knowing who you are in God will allow you to follow the path God has for you sooner than later. Ephesians 4:11-12 NIV says, *"So Christ himself gave the apostles, the prophets, the evangelists, the pastors and teachers to equip his people for works of service, so that the body of Christ may be built up."* To find your gifts and callings of God, begin to pray and ask God for insight. There are information and books you can read about the different gifts that may help you to understand better which gift is for you.

HOW I FOUND MY PURPOSE:

I began to thirst for knowledge. I knew God had a perfect plan for my life, according to what the Bible says in the book of Jeremiah 29:11, *"For I know the thoughts that I think toward you, saith the Lord, thoughts of peace and not of evil, to give you an expected end.*" The manner in which I found out the call of God on my life, was when God began to give me dreams. I actually dreamed of a family member's death. That opened my eyes to God in such a deeper way. I never fully understood why God showed me that, but I find comfort in the fact that He showed me because He loved me, and He was giving me the comfort of warning my cousin of what was to come. Although my cousin did not heed the warning, I still experienced the opportunity of having God share this with me, and for that, I am eternally thankful.

So, when this dream came to pass, I began to search out this idea of dreams from God. I began to buy books on seers and dream books to get a better understanding and soon found out that I am called by God to be a prophet. A church I once attended provided surveys to their new members, which breaks down an individual's calling and gifts in God through answering questions in the survey. This was also confirmation for me.

One vital step to finding out your purpose in God is to be in right standing with Him. We must have a prayer life, be in fellowship and communion with God on a regular, consistent level. As you pray to God and let Him know your desire to fulfill your full potential in Him, He will begin to open up to you and make His plan for your life evident to you. Once you know this, it will give you much clarity on who you are and why you act the way you do.

RECEIVE WISDOM FROM GOD

In Matthew 25, we learn the story of the wise and foolish virgins, who took their lamps and went out to meet the bridegroom. Five of them were foolish, and five were wise. The foolish ones took their lamps but did not take extra oil with them. The wise ones, however, took oil in jars along with their lamps. The bridegroom was a long time in coming, and they all became drowsy and fell asleep. Verses 6-13 says, *"At midnight the cry rang out: Here's the bridegroom! Come out to meet him! Then all the virgins woke up and trimmed their lamps. The foolish ones said to the wise, Give us some of your oil; our lamps are going out. No, they replied, there may not be enough for both you and us. Instead, go to those who sell oil and buy some for yourselves. But while they were on their way to buy the oil, the bridegroom arrived. The virgins who were ready went in with him to the wedding banquet. And the door was shut. Later the others also came. Lord, Lord, they said, open the door for us! But he replied, Truly, I tell you, I don't know you. Therefore keep watch, because you do not know the day or the hour of my return."*

The wise women were prepared; they had their eyes on the prize; they were focused and determined to attend the wedding banquet. The Bible says "wisdom is the principal thing, get wisdom, in all thy getting, get an understanding." We must understand that we do not know the day of our Lord's return, so we must be prepared and ready at all times. Do not believe that at the last moment you can try to straighten out some kinks in your life, and God will receive you, because He will not. Philippians 2:12 says, *"work out your own salvation with fear and trembling."* We must stay in tune with the Spirit of God. We must live a holy life before God as He is holy. We must examine ourselves daily to ensure we are found in the faith.

The foolish women had a few things working in their favor; they were in the right location to meet the bridegroom to attend the wedding banquet. They had their lamps with them just in case they were needed or if the wait was a little longer than expected, and they were virgins which is very honorable. The problem was they didn't take enough oil with them to last the whole night. That is like sitting in your car getting ready to go to work in the morning and not having the keys to drive. Proverbs 14:8 says *"the wise understand where they are going, but fools deceive themselves."*

See, the foolish women were not prepared for where they were going. They had their lamps, but not enough oil to keep the lamps lit. Therefore, when the wise virgins went out to the wedding banquet, the foolish virgins lost focus of the goal and left the scene to go to a store to buy more oil. We are to always keep our eyes on the prize, which is Christ Jesus. When we read our Word and follow His Spirit, we must not get distracted by the things that come along that are not of God.

When the foolish women came to the door and knocked, they were not allowed to come in and feast because they were found to be unworthy. Why? It is just like the story where Jesus walked up to the fig tree when he was hungry and found no fruit on it. The virgins were found to be unfruitful. They had the appearance of being ready and prepared for marriage, but they were not. If they truly spent time in the presence of God, they would have had the wisdom to know to bring oil.

Luke 14:28-30 NIV says, *"Suppose one of you wants to build a tower. Won't you first sit down and estimate the cost to see if you have enough money to complete it? For if you lay the foundation and are not able to finish it, everyone who sees it will ridicule you, saying, This person began to build and wasn't able to finish."* You cannot live your life anyhow and believe that when Jesus returns you will be accepted into His Kingdom.

Foolish women are carried away with the things of the world. They get distracted from the things of God very easily. They hate to be alone in the presence of God but love to be in secular venues with their friends. Foolish women have not learned to tame their tongues even though the Bible says that life and death are in the power of the tongue. Foolish women date any man that passes their surface level test; either he is cute, has a nice car, has a nice job, or nice body. Seek wisdom. Now is the time to seek the face of God; the book of James says that if any man lacks wisdom he is to ask God, and He will give it to him.

The word of God has all of the wisdom keys we need to live a life that is pleasing to God. He tells us how to honor our mothers and fathers. He tells us how to seek wise counsel. He shows us the consequences of sinning and not living a life that gives Him honor. His Word tells us to keep away from the adulterous man and fools. We are taught to follow wisdom. Proverbs 1:23 says "*come and listen to my counsel. I will share my heart with you and make you wise.*"

DISTRACTORS

It is very important to understand Satan's

purpose. His ultimate plan is to get you out of the will of God and on the track of disaster. How does he go about doing this? He does this by sending **distractors** into your life in the form of people, both male and female. According to www.oxforddictionaries.com © University 2016 Oxford Press, **distraction** can be defined as a thing that prevents someone from concentrating on something else.

Satan will send you a best friend who is nice, kind, educated, and fun to hang around, but not living according to the will of God to distract you. Her advice will seem like good advice, but because she does not have any convictions and does not dwell in the presence of God, it will lead you astray. And regarding friends of the opposite sex, Satan will send people into your life just to distract you.

Have you ever dated someone you knew was not at all what you truly wanted, but you would go to the movies with him or talk on the phone with him for hours? I had a male best friend I would go to the gym with; he would hang out at my house, and we would watch television and talk for hours, just wasting time—the time that I could have been doing something productive for God. This was a distraction to keep me off track with God's will for my life.

When you look back at these friendships and relationships, you will realize how many other positive things you could have been doing besides just wasting time. Sometimes, we waste time with people because we think eventually we will win them over for Christ, or because we do not believe they are influencing us. In self-deceit, we may even use the scripture in Proverbs 11:30 that says "he who wins souls is wise" as a crutch to stay in fellowship with these distractors. I can relate to this in that most of my friends are still in the same predicaments they were in before I started hanging out with them. They are still fornicating and have not recommitted their lives to God.

My friends that were not saved watched my lifestyle very carefully, waiting for me to do something ungodly; and they did not necessarily call me on it the first time. It is as if they gathered up their notes and waited for what they felt was a good opportunity to plead their case on how ungodly I was. I was one of those Christians that quoted scripture all the time, prayed, and said, "Lord, Thank You Jesus" all the time, so that was possibly irritating to them, but I did not realize it. I figured because we were friends, I could be myself. God took me through a process of showing me how the friends in my life felt about me, and I allowed him to cut the cords on people I thought I was helping.

We believers who are endeavoring to live right must wake up and realize this walk with Christ is lonely. We cannot hang out with any and everybody doing God knows what and still expect to please God. In Isaiah 29:13, the Bible says, "Therefore, *the Lord said, Forasmuch, as these people draw near me with their mouth, and with their lips, do honour me but have removed their heart far from me, and their fear toward me is taught by the precept of men.*" Most of the people that say they are a believer are only saying it with their mouths and not with their lifestyles. God requires more from us than just lip service. He requires our lifestyles to be an example of what we believe. We must stay on track.

In Matthew 10:16, the Bible says, "*Behold, I send you forth as sheep in the midst of wolves: be ye, therefore, wise as serpents, and harmless as doves.*" When God begins the separation process, it is unnecessary for you to get out of character and act as the world does. You can let friendships and relationships go in a nice, harmless way. If you and a friend are having disagreements, just state the obvious, state your stance on the situation that is causing the confusion, and let them know you no longer have any need for the friendship. It is as simple as that, especially if this is a friendship the Lord wants you to release. Let it go in the Name of Jesus.

By faith, we must walk out the plan God has for us. The plan that God has for us is a holy, righteous plan. God does not take pleasure in us living lives without consideration of Him. The Bible teaches us to *"seek ye first the Kingdom of God and all His righteousness and all these things will be added unto thee"* (Matthew 6:33). We must seek God first. We must not do as the world does. We must live everyday to please God. We are not to be concerned with pleasing ourselves or our friends.

The Christian walk is not a self-pleasing walk. It is a walk that pleases God; it is a sacrificial lifestyle. As we please God by living godly, by reading and applying the Word to our lives, and by fellowshipping with like-minded believers, we set ourselves up for all of the benefits of God. In Psalms 103:2-5, the Bible says, *"Praise the Lord, my soul, and forget not all his benefits—who forgives all your sins and heals all your diseases, who redeems your life from the pit and crowns you with love and compassion, who satisfies your desires with good things so that your youth is renewed like the eagle's."*

I learned to shake off the world's view on love and relationships after my divorce. I was saved when I got married but still had too much of the world's influence on me. I was a complete babe in Christ. I had no one in my family walking after the Spirit of God. I only had friends and family that were carnal/fleshly. When I found God, the first thing I chose to do was "live right" by abstaining from sex, so I got married, completely missing God.

See, God did not just want me to "live right," He wanted me to be right. I walked into a marriage thinking love would hold us over and keep us together, not knowing that what truly holds a marriage together is a marriage founded on the Word of God, blessed by God, ordained by God, destined by God, pleasing to God, and honorable to God.

CHAPTER 4
THE WARNING SIGNS

There were a few signs that appeared when I dated my ex-husband that had I paid attention to, I could have avoided the marriage altogether. Not only were some signs overlooked because I was in love and naïve, but also some signs were missed simply because I did not heed sound advice and counsel from those closest to me.

SOUND ADVICE

Once we were engaged and began to plan for our wedding, my mother told me I should wait. She felt we were in haste and should spend a little more time together before we wed; I did not listen. The number one reason I did not listen was that I did not want to live in sin and shack up; so in my mind, marriage was a good decision. I absolutely did not view my waiting another year before marrying him as an option.

Several days before the wedding, a very good friend of mine took me to church with him. There, an elder shared with me the fact that my fiancé was not truly saved and pointed out to me just how much of a babe I was in Christ. She asked directly, "Is he saved?" I said I did not know, which I knew he was not saved but did not want to feel as though I was judging him. She quoted some scriptures and was asking me to quote along with her, but I had not memorized any scriptures. I do not even think I knew John 3:16 at that time. Had I known the depths of what I was getting myself into, I would have waited; but again, I was in love.

Early on in our relationship, I had a few situations that came up, where others who were not that close to us tried to shine the light on my boyfriend but I did not listen. One female in my command came to me and said my boyfriend was a player; another male at our duty station told me he had a girlfriend before he started dating me. Well, my boyfriend denied this all and told me they were lying on him. So, of course, I never witnessed negative behavior from him, so I did not believe them.

Another sign I received was during a time he was at home visiting his family, and I was talking with his step mom on the phone; she kept calling me another girl's name. I did not know this at the time because he never shared it with me, but he had a girlfriend at home in the states, while he and I were dating overseas. This girl was "waiting for him." Looking back on this now, I see all of these as warning signs that he was no good; but while we were dating, I was naïve and in love, so I did not take heed to them.

SMALL LIES

There were two pure lies he told me at the very beginning of our relationship. The very first time I caught him lying, it was about his age. I was the type of girl who did not like to date older guys. Still to this day, I do not. When I met my ex, and we began to date, I was 18, and my ex told me he was 19; but I found out at a later date he was 20. His excuse was that he forgot he had just had a birthday 2 months prior...but later he explained that he knew if he told me he was 20, I would not have dated him. He was right. Even though that gap does not seem major, I liked guys my own age and it mattered to me.

Then there was a time he lied about purchasing some tennis shoes, and I could not understand why he felt the need to lie. He told me he did not buy anything while out with his friends, but later on, I found out he did. It was a pair of Air Jordan's; I guess there was a reason for him to lie, but I never understood why. I was eventually going to find out what he purchased.

THE FRIEND I NEVER MET

When I dated my husband, I only met one of his childhood friends. The friend I met was a man of God who is now a pastor. Once we were married, I met one of his childhood best friends whom he was very close to. They were like twins; they were the same height, skin tone, and body frame. This friend told me so many things about him I had never heard before...how he was a player in high school. He went on and on talking about how he could not believe he had settled down; and how he used to have all the girls in school; and how he spent all his money on them. He was a ladies' man.

AHHHHH!! At this point, everything was starting to make sense to me, and I believed every word that was coming out of his friend's mouth. This was the first time I heard this news, and it actually registered for me. Now I believed it. After meeting this friend, I knew why I had never met him before; my ex was very sneaky and wise to keep him away from me.

GOD, AM I DATING THE RIGHT PERSON?

THE BIGGEST SIGN I MISSED

Another big eye-opening moment, the one I now feel was the biggest sign of them all, was when my fiancé decided to let me know straight up that he had no intentions of going to church all the time like we did while we dated. I was blown away! Now, there were several times before this that I wanted to call the relationship off, but this-right-here took the cake. I could not believe he just said the Christian life that we were living was not what he wanted. I was mad and ready to call off the relationship as well as the marriage.

So, why did I not break up with him after he made this comment? Danielle, your fiancé just told you he will not be attending church all the time like y'all were doing. He will not be doing that…you are about to bounce on this relationship, right? How can two walk together unless they agree? Do not be unequally yoked together with unbelievers?

WRONG…what went wrong was I got advice from an unwise friend who meant well.

At the time, I explained what happened to one of my best friends, the fact that my fiancé bluntly and seriously told me that when we get married, he will not be attending church the way I was. I was heated and ready to call everything off. But, my good friend, who was the only person I talked to about this, told me that my fiancé loved me and that he was just upset. My friend said, "The devil had gotten into him and made him say that, and he did not really mean it." So, I relented. I let my friend's words calm me down, and I accepted my fiancé's apology. IF I COULD TURN BACK THE HANDS OF TIME...

DO NOT MISS GOD

Missing God and being involved with the wrong person, will throw you out of the right season and the will of God. Missing God means He has something better for you, but for some reason, you chose to do something different. How do you know you have missed God in a decision that you made? You will have no peace and feel disconnected from the Spirit of God. You will have a knowing in your spirit that the relationship you are in is not right in the eyes of God.

There is no feeling worse than realizing you have missed God. I missed God by not abstaining from sex before I got married. I did everything backward as the world does. I had sex, fell in love, got saved, and then got married. In a godly individual who is saved and loves the Lord, we should be saved first, love God with all our heart, date responsibly, submit this relationship to leadership, fall in love, get married, then have sex.

I missed getting the real, deep connection with God because I started the relationship with my boyfriend too soon. I became infatuated and taken away by my sweetheart and did not know anything about fasting. I did not know how to pray for one hour as Jesus commanded His disciples. I had no idea that when you pray to God and He does not respond, you must go deeper in prayer, not give up and make your own choice.

What I needed to do was realize, accept, and repent that I was outside of the will of God for my life in my marriage. How did I know I was outside of the will of God? First of all, my conviction came from all the doubts I had while dating. Also, I was pricked by my husband's direct words to me that he was not going to be into all the church stuff as I was. I needed to repent to God for missing Him at that time in my life. God tried to show me what I was getting myself into. I needed to forgive my husband for his actions. I was not made for him; I was not his rib. We were both out of God's will when we got married. The Bible says how can two walk together except they agree? Well, if two unequally yoked people get married, things like what happened in my marriage begin to happen.

THE WARNING SIGNS:

The following are warning signs we must heed at inception when getting to know someone:

1. If the man is unrepentant towards God, living in willful disobedience, and has no convictions about the sins that he commits, he is not the one. If he is not saved, then he needs to give his hearts to God before you begin to date exclusively. If you try to date someone who is sinning sexually, pretty soon you will fall into fornication and need an altar call and deliverance from sexual sin. If he believes in God but is not sure about how he feels about Jesus, do not date him. He needs to grow into the things of God and is not the one for you.

2. When you catch a man in a lie, RUN. It does not matter how small. If you stick around, you will soon see that he is hiding really big things from you and they possess a spirit of deception.

3. When he is not sharing about his past relationships and personal life, STOP. If you find yourself doing all of the sharing, pause and learn more about him. Ask questions with the intent to learn the person you are dating. Listen and listen well. A wise woman once told me to always listen to a man talk. She said a man will tell you exactly who he is if you would just listen.

4. When your mother does not approve, STOP. Whether she is a Christian or not, stop because mothers have wisdom—they often speak out of rich experience rather than sentiment. They are the ones that raised you, and you should respect their opinions and take it to God in prayer.

5. If he is not deep in the Lord, STOP. What is his personal relationship with the Lord like? When you find God and have a true personal relationship with Him, it is very important for the person you are dating to have the same relationship. Just going to church is not enough. Praying together is not enough. Does this person pray on his own? Does he go to church without you and read his Bible alone? When was the last time he shared something with you from the Bible that spoke to him?

6. If someone who knows the person you are dating comes to you and shares insight about him, heed that insight. Take it to God in prayer. Pray and fast and ask God for insight on this information that was shared with you. Do not be so quick to tell your significant other what was shared with you, because they will denounce and reject it as irrelevant and untrue information.

Let God know that your desire is not to make a mistake in choosing this person as a spouse. After you have prayed and heard from God, mention it to your partner and wait for a response and an explanation. If his only response is, the person who shared this information with you is lying, that is not a good enough answer. You must weigh the insight that was given to you; if you do not do the work now, you will regret it later.

7. You are a child of God and should not be having sex outside of marriage. If the person you are dating is always talking about sex, pressuring you to have sex, and always pushing up on you, STOP. They are dealing with a spirit of perversion and need deliverance. Do not let them talk you into sex. Birth control or condoms are not necessary in the life of a believer. Sex outside of marriage is a sin. Having sex too soon will cause you to marry for the wrong reason.

8. If your love interest does not attend church regularly or have a church home, STOP! Are you always the one to bring up the things of God or is this a pursuit of his also? The reason people are telling you that you two must be equally yoked is that you do not want to be the person who is always going to church while your spouse and the kids are at home sleeping on Sunday mornings. You do not want to be the only one with a zeal for God; this can be a very lonely place.

9. If he is always talking about his ex-girlfriend, STOP! This is a sign that he is not emotionally healed. Although you may find this individual very suitable for you, trust me, he is not if he has not emotionally taken his mind off the last relationship. Save yourself some heartache and pain and take a step back. Pray for his emotional healing and for God to give him direction and insight.

10. If he is married, separated, or currently shacking up with his significant other, STOP! As a single Christian, you should never be close friends with someone of the opposite sex whose marital status is married or separated. It does not matter if you met him before he got married; this is an open door for confusion and deception. If he is married and telling you stories of how unhappy he is, pray for him but do not, under any circumstances, view this man as potential for you, because he is not and will only hurt you in the long run.

Dear reader, please understand there is a great danger in not heeding the warning signs and deciding to move forward with an individual God has not sent to you. Do not give them benefits of doubt. Do not feel that this person may wake up tomorrow and realize you are the one. If the person you are dating has shown you numerous signs that they are not in alignment with God's will for their life, how can they be the one for you? God will not send you a mate in the form of a "science project." God does not want you to build a man; that is not His will for you. You must have faith to walk away and continue to seek God's desires for you. If the individual you are dating has shown you any of these signs, please stop dating him and reconnect and resubmit to God. You will save yourself a lot of heartache and pain.

CHAPTER 5
ARE YOU READY?

Samson's story is told in the book of Judges Chapter 13-15. Samson's parents were believers and deeply in tuned with God. An angel appeared to his mother to let her know she was no longer barren and would carry a child, and that her son was going to be a Nazarite to God (Numbers 6:1-21), from the womb, who would begin to deliver the Israelites from the Philistines. The Bible says that the Lord blessed Samson and the Spirit of the Lord began to move upon him.

You would think a child who was blessed by God from his mother's womb and had godly parents would grow up and do the will of God all the days of his life...WRONG. In chapter 14, we get right into Samson's love life and find out the type of women he was attracted to. Verse 1 says Samson went down to Timnah and saw a Philistine woman he wanted to marry. He took his desires to his parents and his father immediately asked him, is there no woman among the daughters of your brethren or all of my people that you can take as a wife? Samson wanted what he wanted, so they got the young woman for him; she pleased him well.

There came a time when the Philistine men came to Samson, and they placed a bet. Samson told them a riddle, and if they guessed correctly, he would give them winnings and vice versa. On the seventh day, the men could not solve the riddle, so they went to Samson's wife and threatened her for the answer, so she turned against Samson. They asked her for the answer to the riddle; she cried and cried and accused Samson of not loving her for 7 days until he gave her the answer. She gave the Philistines the answer and they won the bet. Samson's wife was given to one of his companions.

In Chapter 16:1, he was sleeping with a prostitute named Delilah, and by verse 4 he had fallen in love with her. The rulers of the Philistines went to her and said, "See, if you can lure him into showing you the secret of his great strength and how we can overpower him, so we may tie him up and subdue him, each one of us will give you eleven hundred shekels of silver."

For each woman he got involved with that was not of his kindred, he had a great battle to fight. Each woman had something to gain by sleeping with Samson and getting close to him, but Samson never learned. He never took it seriously that these men were out to kill him and were using the women to get to him. John 10:10 says, *"The thief comes only to kill, steal, and destroy, but I have come to give you life and that more abundantly."* A life decision for Samson would have been him listening to his parents and dating a woman of his kind (Proverbs 1:8-9). But he did not. He continued to walk the road that led to death and destruction, never understanding just how bad things were.

With us, a lot of times, we find ourselves in cycles, either dating the same type of people or going around in circles with one person who will not honor us. We are to learn from Samson's tragic story and take heed to the word of God. Proverbs 16:25 says, *"There is a way that seemeth right unto a man, but the end thereof is the way of death."* Samson knew his purpose; he knew God was with him in each battle. In Judges 15:18, he spoke to God directly about the victory he just accomplished to the glory of God and asked God for water, which He provided him.

Why was he so disobedient and why did he allow his lust for the wrong types of women to be his demise? Why do we date and marry the wrong people and allow the relationship with them to be our spiritual demise? The answer is because we are rebellious, and this blatant rebellion brings us outside of the will of God. We want what we want by any means necessary. We lust after relationships and marriages and place God on the back burner.

Delilah was the death of Samson; he told her the secret to his strength. The rulers of the Philistines captured him and threw him in prison, where he was still fighting the men until his end. From Samson, we learn the importance of giving our lives to God before we give our hearts to man. The Bible says that God knows the secrets of the heart. Since God knows the secrets of the heart, we need to put our trust in Him. We do not have to go through the struggles that Samson encountered. In the book of James, the Bible says if any man lacks wisdom, let him ask of God. We must trust God, His Word, and godly counsel to make it in this world and not get caught up with a person who was not ordained by God for us.

ACCEPTING MISTREATMENT

A clear sign that you are making wrong decisions in your dating life is that you are not being treated the way the word of God says you should be treated. The Bible says, "*I will praise thee; for I am fearfully and wonderfully made: marvelous are thy works; and that my soul knoweth right well"* (Psalm 139:14). When God created man, He said it was good.

If you are dating a person who treats you any different from this, they are not of God. We are to desire the things that God desires for us. As far as relationships go, you want a relationship with a person that builds you up as God builds you up. If you are being torn down mentally or physically, he is not from God. In John 10:10, the Bible says, *"The thief comes only to steal and kill and destroy; I have come that they may have life, and have it to the full."* Jesus uplifts and encourages us and grants us eternal life when we follow Him.

1 Peter 1:16 says, *"Be ye holy as I am holy."* When we accept the Lord into our hearts, He begins a continual work in us. To be holy, we must look to God, the Author and Finisher of our faith. We must read the Word of God to know what it is that He expects from us. We do not accept God into our lives and automatically become new people; it is a process. Day one of our salvation, we say yes to Jesus. We become saved. Saved means you have died to sin and are making a conscious decision to follow Jesus as a disciple.

When I initially began to date, I was not saved. I did not have the real personal relationship with God that I have today. I just believed in God and went to church. I got truly dedicated before my engagement, and because of that, I made a lot of mistakes and missed God by marrying the wrong person. To have success in dating, it is important to pray to God for wisdom and heed Him in prayer.

I had no one to teach me the ways of a saved, single woman. My problem was that I started dating first and found God later. I did what I knew how to do and what I was taught from society. Society teaches us to date based on how someone looks or their status in society. The Word teaches us to desire to be equally yoked and date someone with a heart for God.

It is very hard to break the cycles that our parents, siblings, friends, and society have set for us. At the end of the day, whether 25, 35 or 45 years old, we find ourselves looking back over our childhood and our parents' mistakes trying to figure out how we got into the mess we are in within our own lives. It is important that we find out as soon as possible if we are dating the person that God has for us.

What we must come to grips with is that we are not the person we have become. There is a war raging on the inside of us, a battle between good and bad, spirit and flesh. Whether you were raised in the church or found the Lord at a later age, we all must begin to pull away from the ways we were raised and our worldly views on relationships and begin to walk in the ways of the

Lord.

To start walking in the ways of the Lord and understanding the ways of God, we must pick up our Bible for example. The book of Proverbs, Romans, and Galatians are very helpful in explaining how we should carry ourselves and behave as Christians.

•Romans 12:1-2 says, *I beseech you, therefore, brethren, by the mercies of God, that ye present your bodies a living sacrifice, holy, acceptable unto God, which is your reasonable service. And be not conformed to this world, but be ye transformed by the renewing of your mind, that ye may prove what is good, acceptable and perfect, will of God.*

•Proverbs 5:1-5 says, *My son, attend unto my wisdom and bow thine ear to my understanding: That thou mayest regard discretion, and that thy lips may keep knowledge. For the lips of a strange woman drop as a honeycomb, and her mouth is smoother than oil: But her end is bitter as wormwood, sharp as a two-edged sword. Her feet go down to death; her steps take hold on hell.*

•Galatians 5:18-21 says, *but if ye be led of the Spirit, ye are not under the law. Now the works of the flesh are manifest, which are these:*

adultery, fornication, uncleanness, lasciviousness, idolatry, wrath, strife, seditions, heresies, envyings, murders, drunkenness, revelings, and such like; of the which I tell you before, as I have also told you in time past, that they which do such things shall not inherit the kingdom of God.

As children of God, it is important for us to shake off all the ways of the world and the things we have been taught by our family members and friends. Once we receive Christ in our hearts, it is important for us to deeply search for godly ways to begin to clean up our thought lives and our actions. The Bible says, *"We are therefore Christ's ambassadors, as though God were making his appeal through us"* (2 Corinthians 5:20). Are your family members and friends saved? I mean really saved? Not just in words, but saved in their lifestyles?

The world has taught us to date the people we find physically attractive or date the people who we believe have the most to offer us. Some of us start dating and having sexual relations as early as age 13. What do we know at the age of 13? I started seriously dating at age 18, and I did not know a thing about what I should have been looking for. I dated guys I was physically attracted to or guys I felt were smart in school. I learned from my family that you need a man with money who could take care of you.

Are the people who have the most influence on you saved? How do you know if they are really saved? Look at their lifestyles. The Bible says in Matthew 7:16 that we will know them by their fruit. What kind of lifestyles do your family members and friends have? Are they living in sin? Do they practice their religion only on Sunday? Do they walk in the fruit of the Spirit? Do they have a prayer life? Are they humble? Are they givers to others like the homeless and fatherless?

We are called to be peculiar and different from the world, our family, and our friends. If our role models and family members are not followers of God and believers of the word, we are not to do the things they do. What do they do? They shack up, they cheat, they lie, they steal, they envy, and they lust. We are people of God. Our walk and our talk should be different. 1 Peter 1:15 says, *"But as He which hath called you is holy, so be ye holy in all manner of conversation."*

The lesson we learn from the world through television and radio is how to fornicate. We pump this worldly music and these worldly behaviors into our psyche so much that we act out the things they teach us. Even though we know sex outside of marriage is a sin, we do it because it seems to come naturally to us. Everyone else is doing it. We see other couples who live together, fornicate, have children outside of marriage, get married and seem happy; so we think it is okay for us to do it too. It is not pleasing to God when we, His children, live these un-yielded, unfruitful lives that give Him no glory.

LET GOD REPOSITION YOU:

"Enter ye in at the strait gate: for wide is the gate, and broad is the way, that leadeth to destruction, and many there be which go thereat. Because strait is the gate, and narrow is the way which leadeth unto life, and few there be that find it," Matthew 7:13-14.

There is a repositioning process with God. We must get off the broad road, which is the way everyone else does things, and make a personal decision to walk the narrow path. As you come to understand the difference between the ways of God and the ways of the world, you must change things about your thought life and your lifestyle. You are presenting your body as a living sacrifice, holy and acceptable to God, which is your reasonable service.

The narrow way is the way to receive the blessings and provisions that God has for your life. Being on the broad way brings on curses and destructions. We can never think this is a walk where we will receive the blessings and good things of God without putting forth any effort.

This is a faith walk, the walk of God is not easy. You must fight daily.

You will have all types of temptations and distractions coming your way, but you must fight. You must push past all circumstances that come your way that are not like God and keep the prize in mind. In Philippians 3:13-14 the Bible says, *"Brethren, I count not myself to have apprehended: but this one thing I do, forgetting those things which are behind, and reaching forth unto those things which are before, I press towards the mark for the prize of the high calling of God in Christ Jesus."*

Never give up on God or your walk in Him. If it seems hard to live right, connect yourself with like-minded individuals and allow the Holy Spirit into your life; He is your Helper. Begin to find out the desires God has for your life. If you are single, God desires holiness and not fornication. Push away from friends that are not walking the Christian walk. They may say that they are, but take a look at their lifestyle and their conversation. If they promote you being promiscuous or sexually active, they are not sent in your life from God, but from the enemy as a distractor. You must push away from them and pray for their salvation in Christ. Staying connected to these types of people will keep you out of the will of God and on that broad road.

The narrow road will be a road where God can

begin to make His plan and purpose for your life known. He will begin to download His instructions and give you insight into your day-to-day life and your future. As you please God with your body and choices, you will find much fulfillment in your relationship with Him. He will talk to you and walk with you; He yearns for fellowship with you and to release great things into your life. Be ready and walk circumspectly before God.

EMOTIONAL WHOLENESS

The Bible says in Matthew 6:22, *"The light of the body is the eye: If therefore thine eye be single, thy whole body shall be full of light. But if thine eye is evil, thy whole body shall be full of darkness. If therefore the light that is in thee be darkness, how great is that darkness."*

It took me a very long time to get over the way I began to view men. My eye had become evil. I saw them all as no good. I saw them all as cheaters. I began to believe they only loved you and were faithful temporarily until the next best thing came along. I had an opportunity to get back with my ex-husband after we had filed for our divorce, but I refused to. I had lost all faith, hope, and trust in him. When I went home to recover, I moved in with my parents. My dad's negative behaviors and actions with other women continued. I unknowingly became cold-hearted and bitter.

An important factor in receiving emotional wholeness is getting rid of the residue in your life. According to www.oxforddictionaries.com © 2016 Oxford University Press, **residue** can be defined as a small amount of something that remains after the main part has gone or been taken or used. After my marriage had ended, I was left with the residual effects of the heartache and disappointments of the relationship not working out. I found myself going around and around in circles for years seeing every man I dated as if he were going to do the same things that my ex-husband did. The man would look nothing like my ex or had none of his similar characteristics, but I was always reminded of my past, and this frightened me and kept me from receiving the very things that I wanted.

I was in desperate need of deliverance to release the hurt and pain of my failed relationship. I divorced my husband, but never fully let go of the hurt and pain he caused me; those feelings were still there within me. I always felt there was something God was trying to say to me by sending me the same type of relationship, but I never understood what I was missing. I was in a rut, but could not figure out what I was doing wrong.

Because I did not totally rid myself of the

residue after my divorce, I had become bitter. I would meet guys I liked but never totally let my guard down. I would anticipate another woman coming on the scene, and when it happened, I just let the man go. I never considered myself to be bitter, but I was. When you feel as if you cannot win for losing, and that you are a good person, then why are you still single and alone? When you also feel that you must be cursed because you have not found someone to love you the way you know you deserve to be loved, it is easy to become bitter. I had hang-ups in my life because I did not fully detach from the effects of the last relationship. Even though the man was no longer physically present in my life, he was there in my soul.

How did I get the residue out of my life? I actually had to have a prophetic woman of God call it out, and God used her to answer my prayers. I had prayed and prayed to God about the issues I had going on but never felt any relief. I eventually began to see myself as the common denominator, so I stopped blaming the guys and calling all of them losers, yet I still did not quite understand what I was doing wrong. I was thinking every guy I dated was going to do the same thing my husband did, so I ran from relationships.

The woman of God who prophesied to me said I had missed God because I vowed never to go through "that again." I never wanted to be hurt again, so I unknowingly never allowed myself to embrace love again. I cried like a baby because she was absolutely right. I thank God I finally got the help I needed. I released all of the hurt, pain, and disappointments that day and never looked back again. I took responsibility for my part in this problem, and I optimistically embraced my future.

If you are constantly replaying old relationships in your mind, comparing your new relationships to that one, past relationship, or if you are still dreaming of that previous mate in your present life, you are not free in your soul; the residue is still there. You are in need of deliverance and must gain freedom from your past. Saying you forgive a person for the wrong they did you is the first step, but that is not all it takes. You must ask God for wisdom and allow Him to bring these issues to the surface in your life, and you must take action by releasing them. So, first begin with prayer; this is vital. Let God know that your desire is to walk whole in Him even as it relates to your heart and emotions and that you want Him to show you the errors you are making when dating.

Removing the residue also includes checking your fruit and the fruit of those around you. If you are going to walk by faith and believe the Lord has a special someone for you, you must believe this in your heart and show it by your actions. This does not only go for you, but for those that are in your company. It makes no sense to believe God for the best but have friends who doubt it, and every time you meet a new person, they are whispering in your ear that it is just a matter of time before you figure out that he is no good. Get these people out of your ear.

STAY IN THE PRESENT

Another important factor in receiving emotional wholeness is for us to stop longing for the relationship that does not exist in our present moment. When a relationship ends, sometimes, in our minds, we spend a lot of time rehearsing what they did, what I did, what we did, and we do it over and over. This is a very bad state of mind, where you may be imprisoned. 2 Corinthians 10:5 says that we are to *"cast down imaginations, and every high thing that exalteth itself against the knowledge of God, and brings into captivity every thought to the obedience of Christ."* We must not allow our minds to wander and wander thinking of our past mistakes, failures, and rejections and we must stop longing for that old relationship or love interest. Do not get stuck in your mind, wishing someone who is no longer present was still with you.

What we have to do is begin to denounce and

reject thoughts of our past relationships. When your ex comes to your mind, say, for instance, it is their birthday, or you pass their favorite restaurant or chill spot, change your thought. Begin to praise God with a worship song or sing in the spirit. Do not sit there and think for long periods of time about your ex, longing and longing for someone in which you are not in a relationship. If he is not there with you today, there is a reason. It is not meant to be. You must release them from your mind. Forgive yourself for your bad actions and decisions that may have caused the relationship to end and look towards your future in God.

It is important to be ready in all aspects of your life, not merely having good credit, or a savings account, or your physical appearance together, but you must also be prepared in your mind and in your heart of hearts, that secret place. Do you believe there is a man who will love you the way that Christ loves the Church? The answer should be yes. If there is any doubt in your heart or mind, please seek God for assurance of His love for you. God loves you so much He sent His Son to die for your sins. You are very valuable and important to God. Luke 12:6-7 says, *"What is the price of five sparrows-two copper coins? Yet God does not forget a single one of them. And the very hairs on your head are all numbered. So do not be afraid; you are more valuable to God than a whole flock of sparrows."*

Why would God punish you and not allow anyone good or righteous into your life? That is a lie from the pits of hell. Allow God to heal your heart and your mind. If the relationship did not work, it is okay. God has a bright future for you, and once you receive the emotional healing that you need, you will be ready to love the right man as God will have you love him. Do not beat yourself up or feel bad about your current condition. It is our process called life, and in the real world, we all can gather baggage along the way. It is all good. Keep your trust and faith in God and allow God to restore you back to your healthy place.

FORGIVE OTHERS

According to www.oxforddictionaries.com © 2016 Oxford University Press, **forgiveness** is when you stop feeling anger towards someone who has done something wrong or you stop blaming someone. When relationships end, it is vital for us to forgive and let it go. Forgiveness means I will not hold a grudge because of something that was done to me. If you were betrayed, backstabbed, or lied on, you'd have to let it go. The Bible says in Philippians 3:13-14 NIV, "Forgetting what is behind and straining toward what is ahead, I press on toward the goal to win the prize for which God has called me heavenward in Christ Jesus."

My healing process began when I started dealing with the issues I had with my father, my ex-husband, and myself. I needed to gain understanding and walk in forgiveness. In the book of Matthew chapter 18 verse 21 & 22, Peter came to Jesus and said, *"Lord, how oft shall my brother sin against me, and I forgive him? Till seven times? Jesus saith unto him, I say not unto thee, until seven times but, until seventy times seven."*

Growing up, my dad was a ladies' man. So, when I got married, I chose a ladies' man, not on purpose, but by nature. When my ex-husband began to act the way my dad did, something rose up on the inside of me that absolutely was not going to allow me to put up with that mistreatment. I saw my mother suffer through my dad's adultery with so much hurt and pain and I did not want to go through that.

For me to get past this mountain of hurt in my life and walk in forgiveness towards my dad and men, I needed to be reminded that none of us are perfect (Romans 3:10). God gives all of us grace. God understands who we are and why we do the things we do.

Firstly, my dad deserved forgiveness from me as Jesus forgave those sinners who crucified Him.

Jesus said to forgive them, for they know not what they do. See, my dad was not a Christian; he never knew his father, and his mother was not saved. So, how can a man love his wife as Christ loves the church if he is not saved and if he did not have a godly example growing up? My dad is not perfect; he is not God.

Secondly, I had to forgive myself for my bad decision. I chose to marry my husband, despite all of the warning signs I received while we were dating. A lot of it was me being naïve and some of it was me just simply not listening. I have learned to forgive myself for my bad decision.

Thirdly, I needed to forgive my ex-husband. His childhood was rough. He was raised by a mother with a drug addiction. His father was a player and set a bad example for him, which entailed multiple women and adulterous relationships. At the time we met and dated, he did not know any better. He was acting out the things he saw in his life. Yes, he promised to love me and treat me right, but without a true, deep relationship with God, he was doomed to failure and sin. I needed to forgive him, and I have done so.

Finally, I had to extend forgiveness to some of the men I dated throughout my single years for the things they did that hurt me, even unknowingly at times. I got tangled up in some messy situations, like dating and falling for a guy that was not over his daughter's mom; I had received warning signs but still dated him. I had to forgive a guy I dated who played with my emotions and never told me he was living with someone whom he later married.

I had to ask God to help me forgive the men I dated who were simply not ready to commit to me, but said they were so that they could get closer to me. To do this, I had to forgive as Jesus forgave, while He was on the cross being crucified (Luke 23:34). I had to forgive these men because they did not know the amount of pain they were causing me.

See, in God, we learn how to apply wisdom and understanding. God wants us to view things the way He sees things. God is so loving and patient with us, and that is what I needed. The Bible says in Lamentations 3:22-23, *"It is of the Lord's mercies that we are not consumed, because his compassions fail not. They are new every morning: great is thy faithfulness."* In God, we must forgive. If we do not forgive others, God cannot forgive us.

It is hard sometimes to forgive, but forgiving others is a requirement. Even if it takes you 20 years to forgive, you must forgive them. If you are angry with someone, who hurt you, talk to God about it. Let God know how you feel. Give your cares to the Lord. As you give it to God, He will lead you to pray for them. Pray for their salvation; pray for their well-being. Give your hurt to God. Ask God for wisdom to cope with your pain.

Today, I forgive my father for being ignorant in his actions. I forgive my ex-husband for not loving me as Christ loved the church. I ask God to forgive me of my shortcomings and to have patience with me as I walk this walk. Love is a beautiful thing when it is the will of God. There is protection and safety in God; there is peace in God; there is love in God. Without God, we have nothing.

LOVE

1 Corinthians 13 is one of my favorite chapters of the Bible. In verse 3, it says, *"If I give away all I have, and if I deliver up my body to be burned, but have not love, I gain nothing."* Love is a requirement; it comes from the most genuine place in your soul—having love for all people, not just those who love you, but also for those that do not love you. In regards to those who do not love you, you may consider them an enemy, but are they really your enemy? According to www.oxforddictionaries.com © 2016 Oxford University Press, an **enemy** can be defined as a person who is actively opposed or hostile to someone or something.

In matters of the love, a person that does us wrong in a relationship is not our enemy. The fact that the relationship did not work out just means it was not meant to be. He is not the person God has for you. It was not the will of God for you. What you are required to do now is love. Do not reject love. You never know when your good thing from God is going to come. If you hold on to your hurt and pain from your failed relationship, you will be closed off to love when it presents itself.

You cannot look at every new person like the last person that hurt you. People are not all the same. If you were cheated on, allow yourself time to heal and understand that it was something about him that caused him to be unfaithful, not you. Because he is not faithful to God, he can never be fully committed to you. Make sure the next person you date has a genuine connection with the Lord; that way, they will love you the right way and be faithful.

Do not take your failed relationships personally. Do not allow one failed relationship to set the tone for how you view yourself. You are beautiful; you are loved of God; you are unique and special. There is something for you to learn from each failed relationship. Think about it. What were the signs you missed that, had you paid attention to at that time, you would not have gotten so heartbroken? Release all of the wrongs that were done to you.

Verse 5 of 1 Corinthians 13 says, "*It does not dishonor others, it is not self-seeking, it is not easily angered, it keeps no record of wrongs.*" Love keeps no record of wrongs that were done. Wow! This means to stop holding on to past hurts. According to www.oxforddictionaries.com © 2016 Oxford University Press, **disappointment** can be defined as the feeling of sadness or displeasure caused by the nonfulfillment of one's hopes or expectations. In relationships, we hope for the best. We are hoping for long-lasting love and happiness. But how do we react when this does not occur? A lot of us shut off our emotions. We begin to date just for sex or companionship but have no intentions on loving again from the same place we did previously. Why?We are keeping records of the wrongs that were done to us. The Bible says hope deferred makes the heart sick. How many of us have a sick heart? I know a lot of us have been hurt more than once while in love. Some instances may not be as drastic or damaging as others, but hurt is hurt.

It is important after each relationship to take a step back from the relationship and give yourself time to heal. This is the time when you are to get with God and ask Him to heal you. Let God direct and lead you to His perfect will for your life. You may need to abstain from dating for a season and just pour into your relationship with God. God has some things He may need to do in you before your next relationship; it is important for you to let Him have His way.

WAITING ON THE LORD

Realizing that you have been doing things all wrong and you need to surrender to God is not the end of the world. Trusting in God to work things out for you is the best choice and an easy decision. The Lord knows how to send Mr. Right(eous) into your life. You must surrender the way you have been doing things, the types of men you have been dating, the sex outside of marriage, and the beautification process the world teaches us by being more concerned with our outward beauty instead of our inward beauty.

Genesis 24 reveals the story of Abraham praying to God for a wife for his son Isaac. He had a specific woman in mind for his son; a woman of his kindred, a fellow believer, not a woman from Canaan who can be seen as a woman of the world. Abraham sent his servant out to find a wife for his son; while the servant was out searching, he prayed to God and said, *"O Lord God of my master Abraham, I pray thee, send me good speed this day, and shew kindness unto my master Abraham. Let it come to pass that the damsel to whom I shall say, let down thy*

85

pitcher, that I may drink, and she shall say, Drink, thereby shall I know that thou hast shewed kindness unto my master.

"And it came to pass before he had done speaking, that, Rebekah came out, who was born to Bethuel, son of Milcah, the wife of Nahor, Abraham's brother, with her pitcher upon her shoulder. And the servant ran to meet her, and said, let me, I pray thee, drink a little water of thy pitcher. And she said, Drink my lord: and she hasted, and let down her pitcher upon her hand and gave him drink." Rebekah was the one God had for Isaac; and when the two of them met, it was love at first sight, and they were instantly married.

From this story, we learn to be patient and allow the Lord to send us our mate. Rebekah was busy living her life with her family and did not have a care in the world. We are told to be concerned with the things of the Lord when we are single. These things include: finishing our education, figuring out the will of God for our lives, fulfilling our purpose in ministry, and maybe doing a little volunteer work in something that helps the homeless, the fatherless, or the elderly. Waiting on God means not being gullible and believing that every guy you meet is "the one."

Waiting on God to send your spouse means you *wait*—that is, you are prayerful, you are living in expectation of meeting him, but you are not consumed with this. Isaiah 34:16 says, *"Not one shall lack their mate."* God has someone for each of us. Our job is to seek God first and let everything else fall into place. God loves us and wants us to use our faith that He will send us the right person for us in His time.

REMAIN IN EXPECTATION

To live in expectation means you wake up every morning thanking God for your blessings and your miracles. If you have not received the things you believe God for, you must remain in expectation. According to www.oxforddictionaries.com © University 2016 Oxford Press, **expectation** can be defined as a strong belief that something will happen or be the case shortly. You are to be alert and aware of God presenting to you what you desire. This may be presented in a dream, vision, in your hearing, or in your spirit. Write down your desires; talk to God about the spouse you want; keep it in the forefront of your mind. This way, when the miracle, in form of your spouse comes, you are ready.

Keeping it in the forefront of your mind will keep you from entertaining the wrong man. Not being in expectation will cause you to miss out on opportunities that God may be presenting to you. If you wake up in the morning without God on your mind, then when your potential husband crosses your path, you will miss him. God blesses us when we are prepared, and one of my favorite quotes is from Mr. Bobby Unser, who said: "Success is when preparation and opportunity meet."

HAVE FAITH IN GOD

"Now faith is the substance of things hoped for, the evidence of things not seen" (Hebrews 11:1). With dating, we must have faith in God and allow Him to order our steps, where it concerns our mate. God will provide for us, but we must have faith to walk according to His will for our lives and not entertain the wrong man. Be encouraged that as you align your life with the Word of God, He will reward you. Hebrews 11:6 says, *"He is a rewarder of them that diligently seek him."* Seek God with all of your heart and minds; make your request known to Him that you desire a godly spouse, and He will direct your steps. Remain in expectation of God performing this miracle in your life; He will not let you down.

CHAPTER 6
WARNING

When asking God the question, "am I dating the right person?" please make sure you are ready for the answer. God will begin to show you exactly who the person you are dating is and He will not hold back. If he is the person you are supposed to be connected to, give glory to God. If not, be prepared to let go.

In life, there are many different types of people and relationships that we will encounter. We must be able to decipher who these individuals are below the surface and if they were sent from God or Satan. When people see you and show interest in you, you must determine their purpose for wanting to date you and be in your company. Are they in your life to grow with you or take from you?

APPEARANCE OF EVIL

I believe when you come into contact with the person God has for you, He will let you know this is the one. You will know in your spirit. So, if you are seeing someone and it has not been confirmed yet that they are the one, do not act like they are your spouse. Do not, under any circumstance, put yourself in a compromising position.

Do not invite him over to your home after hours. People like to cuddle and things like that, but believe me when I say, cuddling leads to other things. Having at-home movie dates will lead to someone possibly falling asleep and this can lead to problems. Why cuddle and spend time alone with someone who is not your spouse? This is not the behavior of a believer waiting for God to send their spouse.

Ephesians 6:10 says, *"Finally, my brothers, be strong in the Lord, and in the power of his might."* Being strong in the Lord means that you will give your weaknesses and loneliness over to God. When you are lonely, let God know. When you feel weak, let God know. This is not the time to invite the opposite sex over to your home for companionship. God is your spouse while you are single, engage Him in conversation. He is waiting to hear from you.

How should Christians who are waiting for their spouse act? You are the bride of Christ, and you are always to remember Christ's presence; He is always in our midst, never forget this. God sees and knows all and in every conversation and situation which you find yourself, remember the Lord is there too. Do not engage in ungodly conversations or activities; these include bars, clubs, lounges, ungodly music, sleepovers with those that are not your spouse, and cooking and inviting him over for entertainment.

If you are living in the same house with your significant other today, MOVE OUT. You have had enough time and opportunities to hear from God if this is the man God wants for you. If you cannot afford the rent on your own, downsize. Stop making excuses and live right before God. The only way God will send you the person He has for you is if you are obedient to His desires. You are not your own person. 1 Corinthians 6:19-20 says, *"Do you not know that your bodies are temples of the Holy Spirit, who is in you, whom you have received from God? You are not your own; you were bought at a price. Therefore, honor God with your bodies."*

STRADDLING THE FENCE

Please, avoid the man who is on the fence in his relationship with God. I call them men for ministry. They come into your life for you to share your Christian values and faith with only; you are not to get into a relationship with them. He will be weak in his personal walk with God but may appear to be strong in his words or faith because many of them can quote a scripture or two and will tell you how they pray and believe in God.

These men for ministry may also appear to be the kind of person you want and desire, but remember, Satan has watched you, he has heard your prayers and he knows you very well. Please, understand that he will send what appears to be the perfect person, who is very pleasing to your eyes and sometimes pleasing to your ears. They may go to church when you first meet them but do not get excited. My advice is to give it at least 3 to 6 months of watching their behavior and character.

An individual for ministry may smoke weed, drink alcohol, hang out in bar rooms or clubs, fornicate, and hardly ever speak of the things of God because it is not truly in their hearts. Keep your distance and stay connected to your church family and the things of God. I once met a man who told me he received a vision from God that we were going to work in ministry together and then get married.

When I looked at the man, I was not attracted to him but was honestly thinking, maybe we will have a few things in common, one of the biggest being God. He asked me if I had a church home, I said no. I told him I am looking for a ministry to help me grow in my gift. He asked me for a date and immediately started talking about a future with me.

On our first date, he sat across the table from me holding my hands; then he sat next to me putting his arms around me and was hugging me all on the first date. Our conversations got worse and worse, because the more time we spent together and talked on the phone, the filthier his thoughts became. He was clearly only looking for sex, but was a preacher and bragged about how God called him since he was a child. I was dumbfounded.

When I tried to break things off with him, he tried to latch onto me, but I stayed firm in my belief that God requires holiness from us. He felt I was self-righteous and judgmental and even rebuked me. After talking to him and constantly correcting him about his bad behavior, I decided this person was not from God but was a man that truly needed repentance. The problem was, he was not going to repent of his fornication, because he felt God understood and that sex outside of marriage was permissible. I had to disconnect from him and pray for his soul.

When we encounter men who are not in tune with God, we must give them to Jesus. Praying for them is the best thing we can do and please, do not ever feel you can change them. We must continue to tell them of our stance on sexual purity whenever that issue comes up and how God feels about our sexual sins. This way, we have done our part, whether God sent him in our lives to sharpen them or the devil sent him in our lives to distract us, we come out victoriously.

Another example was with a guy who told me, "I am going to make you break your vow to GOD" WHAT! Of course, he did not tell me this right away but said this after we had been dating for a while. He was the perfect guy on paper: single, business owner, home of his own, nice car, no kids. But of course, I was celibate and not having sex with him. So, one night while talking and watching a movie, this comment of making me break my vow to God slipped out of his mouth.

Now, ladies, we want a man that will encourage us to keep our vow to God to wait until marriage for sex, not someone that will blatantly say, I'm going to make you break your vow to God. Sometimes the best thing we can do for people is praying for them from a distance, and that is exactly what I did. Satan uses anybody he can to take you out of the will of God. **Be careful!**

There is a plethora of people who have married men or women to whom they were not equally yoked, and found themselves in an ungodly union and would give anything to get out. While dating, they had a clue that they were not on the same page, but either the lust of the flesh, the lust of the eyes, or the pride of life got them caught in their emotions. All of us have a worldly list of what we desire in a spouse: he has to drive this type of car, he has to have this type of job, and/or he has to come from this kind of background. All of these attributes have nothing to do with a godly character. We are lusting after a kind of person that we want, and Satan will send this person our way every time.

Then, there will be those who will come into your life to share the Word, their faith, and will encourage you to walk stronger in God. You must understand the difference between these two types of people and remain vigilant and prayerful upon every encounter with the opposite sex. Do not get so distracted by the wrong ones that come into your life that you are emotionally worn out and too tired to notice the right one that will come.

When the right one comes along, he will not have a banner over his head that says *I AM THE RIGHT ONE FROM GOD*. It will be your job to discern and stay on track in your relationship with God. Entertaining the wrong person will cause you to miss God and the one He sends in your life.

YOU HAVE MADE HIM AN IDOL

According to www.oxforddictionaries.com © University 2016 Oxford Press, *idolatry* is extreme admiration, love, or reverence for something or someone. An idol is anything that replaces the One, True God. The Word of God says that we are to have no other gods before Him (Exodus 20:3). In the Bible, Paul says a single woman is to be concerned with the things of the Lord, and the married woman should be concerned with the things that please her husband.

Do you consider yourself to be a person who loves hard? If so, you may be operating in idolatry. When you say you love hard, what you are actually saying is, you have put the good sense the Lord gave you on the shelf, and you will let your heart and emotions be your guide; this is very dangerous. Idolatry in relationships is when you are much more into your significant other than you are obedient to God. No matter how bad the person talks to you or how bad he treats you, you do not leave.

It does not matter how many of your friends say he is not right for you; it does not matter how you have that little voice in the back of your head saying he is not nice since they treat you badly; you wonder if he is the one, you still continue to date him. Do you ever question your worth and value in regards to the person you are dating? As a woman, do you feel like you are pursuing him instead of him pursuing you?

Proverbs 18:22 says, *"Whosoever finds a wife finds a good thing and obtains the favor of the Lord."* The man pursues the woman; so ladies, if the man you are dating is not pursuing you, he is not the one for you, and you are not the one for him. And to the men, a woman should not be running behind you and be proposing marriage to you. You must make a decision on if you feel she is wife material and if she is sent to you from God.

When you are with the person God has for you, the relationship is balanced. You do not cry yourself to sleep at night. All of the people you talk to about your relationship are not asking you, "Why are you still dating that person? You need to leave him; he is no good for you. God has a better plan for you." Isaiah 64:4 NIV says, *"For since the beginning of the world men have not heard, nor perceived by the ear, neither hath the eye seen, O God, beside thee, what he hath prepared for him that waiteth for him."* You must wait on God and give your desires to have a relationship to Him. God has a special person in store that will love and treat you the way Jesus cared for the Church.

DATING FOR CONVENIENCE

In your heart, you have envisioned the man of your dreams, but the individual you are dating does not fit that description. You are simply settling. You are not really happy with the relationship; you are really using them because the one you desire has not come along yet. You need to walk by faith. The one you desire will come, but will he find you caught up with a man you do not want? Being in the wrong relationship will cause you to miss your blessing. You will find yourself on the sidelines later in life wondering why God has not sent you the person of your dreams. Maybe God has sent him, but you were distracted by someone you chose for comfort and convenience, so you missed out.

Think about the last three people you dated, did you feel any of them were sent by God? Were any of them what you desired in your heart as the person of your dreams? You have to grow in the fruit of the Spirit. Have patience with God. Have faith in God. Put your trust in God's ability to give you the desires of your heart.

There are a few different types of people you

will meet, some are for ministry purposes, some are your brothers in Christ that will inspire you to walk stronger in your faith, and some are for marriage. Do not miss God. Discern who these people are as they cross your path. Some are just for you to encourage and inspire them to be the person God has called them to be. Some will encourage you. Ladies, one will see you and know you are his wife and you will know he is your husband. Be encouraged and be ready.

A FORM OF GODLINESS

The truth of the matter is most people desire sex. The difference between a saved and an unsaved person is the unsaved person does not have godly convictions when it comes to their sex life. An unsaved person will speak of the Bible and maybe even go to church, but when it comes to his sex life and having sex whenever and with whoever he wants to, he will do it. If you date this unsaved person, he will want sex from you and may potentially be a stumbling block for you.

A saved person will desire sex, but would not dare cross that boundary. He is a man of God who loves God too much to sin against Him, and he respects himself and you. The saved person will pray with you and for you. The saved person will have keen, godly vision for his life and will endeavor to see if you fit into that vision.

If you are single, saved, sanctified, and presenting your body as a living sacrifice to God, it is going to be hard to find someone doing the same thing. You, as well as the person who peeks your interest, must be in control of your flesh. With over ten years of dating experience, I know that most people have not crucified their flesh. Most people feel they are Christians; they go to church, they pray, but they are still sexually active. In actuality, these people are backsliders and unrepentant of that sin. Sex outside of marriage is not right in the eyes of God and that individual needs to come to a place of repentance regarding their fornication. 2 Timothy 3:1-5 says, *"But mark this: There will be terrible times in the last days. People will be lovers of themselves, lovers of money, boastful, proud, abusive, disobedient to their parents, ungrateful, unholy, without love, unforgiving, slanderous, without self-control, brutal, not lovers of the good, treacherous, rash, conceited, lovers of pleasure rather than lovers of God— having a form of godliness but denying its power. Have nothing to do with such people."*

As we walk out this single walk, we will find a lot of people with the form of godliness, but when it comes to sex, they deny the power thereof. The Holy Spirit gives us the power to live right.

You must be diligent and cognizant of whose company you are keeping. Some people may not have self-control as you do, so you must keep your distance. When involved with an unsaved person, you will surely be tempted. They may let you know upfront what their desires are, but not everyone is straightforward. You must abstain from the appearance of evil and not allow yourself to get caught up in a compromising situation.

Do not take your dating life and your saved walk lightly. Do not think that everyone has the same standards and heart as you do towards God. You, as the saved, sanctified child of God, must keep yourself pure. Jude 1:24 says, *"To him who is able keep you from stumbling and to present you before his glorious presence without fault and with great joy."* You must desire to be a kept woman of God. God will not make you abstain; it is your decision. You must determine with every part of your body, your mind, your will, and your heart that you will not participate in sexual sin.

When you are dating a man and you realize he desires sex with you, this should be a **RED FLAG**. You must be careful when talking and interacting with this individual. If he admits to just leaving a sexually active relationship or if they were just living with someone, **BE CAREFUL**. They must repent of their sin of fornication before you consider them as a potential mate. If you do not tread lightly, you will regret it. God must have this man's heart 100% before you get it.

You do not have to stop all communication, but be strong in your stance on celibacy and abstinence until marriage. Make sure it is very clear that you are saving yourself and have no intentions on sexually pleasing anyone whom you are not married to. If this causes the friendship to end, let him go because they were not sent to you from God. The one God sends to you will ABSOLUTELY wait for you.

If the person you are dating decides to abstain with you, they should repent and understand their need for God (this is the job of the Holy Spirit). You do not want to become their preacher or lecturer, so allow God to move in his heart. We are told to win them with our character, not our words (1 Peter 3:1).

THE CHAMELEON

Believe it or not, there are people in this world who will change their behavior and attitude towards certain things just to get closer to you. If you like horseback riding or opera music, so does he once he has met you. I have talked to men who, at the beginning of us dating attended church, quoted scriptures, talked about the things of God, tried to sound all deep and spiritual; then as time went by, all that stopped.

What these men fail to realize is that in time, the truth will come out. This is why we must be patient and get to know him. A person can only keep up a facade for so long. We, children of God, must be prayerful and alert to see the lies and games that people play. Do not be deceived by their false motives and actions.

It is important to hold back some of your information while you are dating. Ask the guy you are talking to some questions about himself. Do not be so quick to tell him every single detail about your life. Find out his interests and hobbies, who his friends are, what he likes to do on the weekends, and about the type of household in which he was raised. These are all questions that will help him open up in a friendly, warm conversation; it will get him to be honest with you about who he truly is.

Many men I talked to over the years have lied and been deceptive about who they "really are." I had a guy friend who did not believe in Jesus but was dating a girl who did believe and he refused to tell her his truth because he knew she would dump him. They eventually broke up, but he knew this truth would never sit well with her, so he did not tell her.

To avoid these chameleons, we must keep our fellowship and relationship right with the Lord.

We must continue to pray for wisdom and discernment in every friendship and always keep God first in our lives. Allowing God to guide and enlighten us will keep us from being misled. The truth of these people's character will be exposed, and we will be free to make the decision that is best for us.

MARRIED, SEPARATED, OR ENGAGED PEOPLE

Do not ever go on a date with a married person. No matter: if they are from your past and they claim to be unhappily married, if you were high school sweethearts, or they are your co-worker, do not entertain them. If he is married, he is off limits for friendship. You will not wait for their marriage to end and you will not be his shoulder to cry on. This is a demonic connection, and God will not bless this relationship.

For those that are separated from their spouses or going through a divorce, please do not date them. God can move in the woman's heart, and reconciliation can take place; you do not want to be in the way of something that God wants to do in their marriage. Avoid those that are separated or going through a divorce as you would the plague.

A lot of married people go after singles very strongly because there are a lot of unsaved, singles who date them. This is an ungodly gesture and beliefs like this need to be checked and given over to God. If you find yourself being hit on a lot by married people, pray about it. This is from Satan, and he is testing you. Ask God to give you strength to continue standing for godliness and stand your ground. Dating and being friends with married people should never be named among Christian singles.

BESTFRIENDS WITH YOUR EX

When you have dated someone and realized they are not the one for you, you must let the friendship/relationship go. If you do not, that person will become a place holder. Place holders are men you have placed in the position of a friend, but he desires more than a friendship with you. These are people you were once dating, but for some reason, you have chosen not to move forward romantically. This man does not fit the bill of what you truly desire in your heart for a spouse.

If you are single, you should not be entertaining any person of the opposite sex who is not marriage potential for you. Entertaining men whom you are not interested in romantically causes confusion, blockage, heartache, and pain. Seeing and spending time with a person you are not truly interested in holds the spot in your life that should be reserved for your future spouse. If you are single, you should not be getting dressed up going on dates or staying up all hours of the night on the phone with those that are just place holders.

In defense of the place holder, how fair is it for him to spend money on you and time with you that is going nowhere? You are using them as a "best friend" until the one you truly desire comes along. And what will you do with the place holder when the new person comes along? Will you just drop him like a bad habit? If you tell the new date about the place holder, this may cause confusion because you were once in a relationship with the place holder.

The place holder deserves to be treated with respect, and once you get to the point in your relationship that you feel he is not the one, you should politely let them know your feelings and how you will pray fervently that they find the one who is fit for them soon. This may take a minute for you both to adjust, but please cut the tie. Holding on to this friendship is very unhealthy and unwise.

CURSES ON YOUR BLOODLINE

There is such a thing as generational curses. Generational curses in our lives happen when we are subject to certain activities because of the sinful activities of our parents or grandparents. We are subject to unfortunate activities because of our family members' sins. To figure out if this is operating in our life, we must study our family's history and pray to God for revelation and insight. We need to be aware of patterns in our family history like multiple divorces, adulterous affairs, promiscuous lifestyles, addictions, ungodliness, and other sins.

The Bible speaks about generational curses in Numbers 14:18, *"The Lord is slow to anger and abounding in steadfast love, forgiving iniquity and transgression, but he will by no means clear the guilty, visiting the iniquity of the fathers on the children, to the third and the fourth generation."*

Exodus 20:5 says, *"You shall not bow down to them or serve them, for I the Lord your God am a jealous God, visiting the iniquity of the fathers on the children to the third and the fourth generation of those who hate me."*

Exodus 34:7 says, *"Keeping steadfast love for thousands, forgiving iniquity and transgression and sin, but I will by no means clear the guilty, visiting the iniquity of the fathers on the children and the children's children, to the third and the fourth generation."*

Deuteronomy 5:9 says, *"You shall not bow down to them or serve them; for I the Lord your God am a jealous God, visiting the iniquity of the fathers on the children to the third and fourth generation of those who hate me."*

The first part of the cure is the revelation of the curse; secondly, acknowledge it; thirdly, repent, not only for your activity in the curse, but also for your family members who may have knowingly or unknowingly participated in that sin; and finally, stop participating in the behavior and close the door.

When the curse is revealed, it may shock you. For me, it was choosing a man with the same spirit as my dad, an unfaithful and adulterous spirit, not only dating him but also marrying him. I was naïve at the time and a babe in Christ, so I did not know much about generational curses. After years of dating men with the same spirit, I began to see (acknowledge it as) a common trait. Something was attracting these men to me, but I had no idea how to stop it.

Once I realized what was going on, I began to repent and plead the blood of Jesus over my bloodline. I repented of all of my sexual sins from my very first act of disobedience and repented on behalf of all sexual sin of my parents, grandparents, and ancestors. I asked God to cleanse my life and allow me to walk in wholeness before Him. I canceled every activity from Satan and every wicked spirit that was operating in my life.

After this, what I needed to do was to watch out for this wicked spirit/behavior from the beginning of courtship and cut it off at the root. I had to stop entertaining men who were a part of this curse and living in active disobedience to God. The way the curse continues to operate in your life is with sin. If you are participating in any sin, you are allowing the devil to have access into your life. He has an open door and will use it as often as he likes.

When you pray to God about the generational curses that may be operating in your life, be open to the insight He shares with you. When it comes to light, you must acknowledge it. Being naïve will keep you in bondage. Thinking that because you are a child of God and have accepted Jesus Christ into your heart, that a curse will not affect you, is a false belief. Truly, you are saved, but there may also be a curse operating in your life. Ask God for revelation and stay prayerful.

CHAPTER 7
STRUGGLES AFTER THE BREAKUP

THE IDLE MIND

After a breakup, it is very hard to keep the person off your mind. Dreams and memories bombard your thought life. It is like having a wound that will not heal. Each time your ex contacts you be it via text, email, or a phone call, it can make you question and possibly alter your decision. If you talk to him, he may try to find out why you are being distant and what he did wrong. You already know he is not the one for you, be strong and completely detach. You must renew your mind daily with the Word of God, ignore their calls and messages. Push pass this!

Colossians 3:1-3 NIV says *"Since, then, you have been raised with Christ, set your hearts on things above, where Christ is, seated at the right hand of God. Set your minds on things above, not on earthly things. For you died, and your life is now hidden with Christ in God."* It may seem that getting over this relationship is easier said than done, but you must place your affections and thoughts on God. This is done by getting into the Word of God, by praying and worshipping God. When you sense your mind wandering back to old memories, think on the things of God. Do not allow yourself to feel overwhelmed. God is your source of strength; when you feel you cannot take it anymore and you become tired and weary, find yourself in the things of God. This will give you the strength to persevere.

Surround yourself with those that will encourage you and support your decision to walk away from the relationship. Receiving support from those around you will help a lot. If your family and friends understand your walk with God, and they know the reason you are leaving the relationship, whenever you begin to doubt your decision and reminisce on the good times, they will be able to keep you on track and out of trouble.

When your family and friends are against your decision to walk away from the relationship, or if they give you their advice to return by saying things like maybe he will change, shut out their voices. You may only need to cut off their influence for a season, but doing so will be extremely important until you to hear your next move from God.

Matthew 10:34-39 says, *"Do not suppose that I have come to bring peace to the earth. I did not come to bring peace, but a sword. For I have come to turn a man against his father, a daughter against her mother, a daughter-in-law against her mother-in-law—a man's enemies will be the members of his own household. Anyone who loves their father or mother more than me is not worthy of me; anyone who loves their son or daughter more than me is not worthy of me. Whoever does not take up their cross and follow me is not worthy of me. Whoever finds their life will lose it, and whoever loses their life for my sake will find it."*

When it appears that no one understands your walk with God, remember that God understands. Stop seeking approval and acceptance from man and seek the face of God. Romans 17:28 says, *"For it is in Him we live, and move, and we have our being."* When we line our life up with God's will and seek His approval, He takes pleasure in this and will reward us. We must continue to walk by faith.

113

REBOUND

After a relationship ends, it is very important that you take time to heal. The healing process can be very long and extended if you jump into another relationship without getting rid of the junk and baggage you have gathered. Taking time to heal involves understanding how and why you ended up in a relationship with a person you should have never been involved with. It involves taking a good, long look at your actions, wrong behaviors, and your mindset on relationships. You need to seek God and pray for understanding and wisdom and receive His insight.

There is danger in rebounding after a relationship. When you rebound, you begin a new relationship without fully getting over the last one. The danger comes in the fact that the new relationship has the potential to take you a step lower than the previous relationship because, without healing, you will go from bad to worse. You begin to sink lower and lower into a pit. The weight of your bad decisions to date an individual who was not sent from God, and then begin a new relationship with another individual who is not sent from God, is heavy. You begin to deal with things like depression, worry, confusion, stress, heartache, and misery. This is because you are being pushed further and further away from the presence of God. The person you are dating and spending the most of your time with is not connected to God, so neither will you be connected to God.

When a relationship ends, you need a fresh start. You must know the ways of God to understand how the opposite sex is supposed to treat you. You find this out by seeking God and understanding how He feels about you. You are the apple of God's eye. He laid down His life for you. He would never emotionally or physically abuse you. Lying as well as cheating and abusing is not named among the Names of God. God is a Healer, a Deliverer, a Friend, a Counselor, and a Peace Maker. He would never lie to you, cheat on you, or disrespect you. Getting to know God is the best thing you can do before entering the dating scene.

DON'T LOOK BACK

In Genesis Chapter 19, the Bible talks about Lot and his family's escape from Sodom and Gomorrah before God destroyed it. They were given strict orders by the Angels of the Lord to leave and not look back. In verse 16, the Bible says, "*But Lot delayed. So the two men took the hands of Lot, his wife, and his two daughters and led them safely out of the city. So the Lord was merciful to Lot and his family. After they had brought them out of the city, one of the men said, 'Run for your lives! Don't look back or stop anywhere in the valley. Run to the mountains, or you will be destroyed.'"* In verses 23-26, the sun had already come up when Lot entered Zoar. The Lord sent a rain of burning sulfur down from the sky on Sodom and Gomorrah and destroyed those cities. He also destroyed the whole Jordan Valley, everyone living in the cities, and even all the plants. At that point, Lot's wife looked back. When she did, she became a pillar of salt.

When God delivers you from a wrong relationship or a wrong mindset, it is important to take that deliverance seriously and never look back. It appeared that Lot and his family did not want to be set free from that wicked city. Some of the activities there must have been pleasing and entertaining to them. When God comes into your life and shows you His desires for you and the need for you to live holy before Him, take it seriously, for this is the only way that leads to life. You should take the commandments of God *seriously*.

Why would you desire to live a lifestyle that is contrary to God? Why is it that we are okay being entertained by people whose lifestyles are not pleasing to God and they are actually on their way to hell? Genesis 18:20-21 states, *"Then the Lord said, 'The outcry against Sodom and*

Gomorrah is so great and their sin so grievous that I will go down and see if what they have done is as bad as the outcry that has reached me. If not, I will know.'''

We should be convicted when we are entertained and knowledgeable of sinners' lifestyles. Their actions are not things that we should become accustomed to. God says that their sin was so grievous and awful to Him. Wow, if their sin was grievous to God, shouldn't it have been grievous to Lot and his family? Lot had settled in this city and the sin the people were committing had become familiar to him and his family. It was a regular part of his life now.

When we are in the vicinity of sinners and have been delivered from sinful relationships and lifestyles, we must allow a separation to take place. We should not accept our deliverance from God and still maintain close ties and connections to people whose lifestyles are contrary to His Word. The way you win sinners over is through prayer, not fellowship and dates. In the Bible, Lot tried to offer his daughters over to the wicked men of the city, and they refused. They desired the Angels of the Lord.

This is how a lot of your friends and relatives feel about the things of God. A lot of the time, when you try to share a Word from God or mention the things of God, your friends will dismiss you. They will say things like, "Aw man, here she goes preaching again." They are not ready to receive God when they make comments like this, and this is a very big sign that you are not positively affecting them and you need to separate from them. Staying connected can affect your deliverance.

The separation process will not be easy. The best thing you can do is devote time to God in prayer, crying out for your friends and family members that have not yet received God in their hearts. Sometimes preaching to them will not be the resolve. Although you may passionately want to spread the Word of God to them and show them where the Bible says they are wrong, they might not receive it from you. Accept this if it is the case and pray. Luke 18:1 says that "men ought always to pray and not to faint." Give your family and friends over to God and let Him move in their hearts and minds. Remember, the Bible says, one plants, one waters, but God gives the increase (1 Corinthians 3:7). It is not your job to do all three. Just sow a seed of a kind word or a scripture that shows their actions are not godly and leave it alone. Let God work on them.

Once you have decided to separate and live a lifestyle that is pleasing to God, you may begin to feel like an alien. You may feel guilty about distancing yourself from your friends and loved ones and feel unsure about this being the right, Christian thing to do. 2 Corinthians 5:17 says, *"Therefore if any man is in Christ, he is a new creature: old things are passed away, behold, all things have become new.*" Remember that God has called you out of your past sins and desires you to live holy before Him. The new pastimes you must do are: reading your Word, having fellowship with like-minded believers, praying and having fellowship with God. The old things and wrong choices are behind you; they are a thing of your past.

You are not to engage in sinful lifestyles and activities that promote fornication. If you feel the need to explain yourself, do it. 1 Peter 3:15 says that "*we should always be ready to give an answer to every man that asks you for a reason for the hope that is in you with meekness and fear.*" Answer their questions. No, it is not that you are acting funny with them, but you are beginning to see things the way God sees them, and He is not pleased. Stand firm in the things of God. Understand that God deserves our obedience to His Word and even He gets tired of repeating Himself and having the need to pull you out of the same dead relationships and friendships over and over again.

STAY IN YOUR LANE

2 Corinthians 6-14 says, *"Do not be yoked together with unbelievers. For what do righteousness and wickedness have in common? Or what fellowship can light have with darkness?"* One of my favorite sayings is, "opposites attract, but it is having things in common that will keep us together." I try to stay in my lane as much as possible. Staying in your lane means dating someone with similar beliefs and recreational interests as you. I consider myself to be a good, clean, godly-devoted Christian woman; I do not do drugs and I am celibate.

I also am attracted to men of God, who live a clean, good, godly-devoted, Christian lifestyle. A man in a similar lane as mine will have a relationship with God as I do. I am not expecting a man to be as deep as I am with God, but he cannot be straddling the fence in his personal life with God. He must be abstaining from sex; sleeping around in your single life shows your lack of self-control and your lack of reverence for God and His Word. A man in my same lane means, not going to bar rooms, clubs, or constantly looking for that club type of environment. It is so sad for me to take a drive at nighttime on a Thursday, Friday, or Saturday to see droves of men and women in their 50's standing outside in line to get in a club.

A lot of men in the world are attracted to those of us that are saved because they do not have to worry about us. We are always home, sleeping in our beds, praying, not club hopping, reading our Bibles, and singing worship songs. We are the people of their dreams...a good, wholesome, faithful woman of God. But are they the men of our dreams? In my opinion, men in the world are a nightmare.

I am not attracted to men that are still heavily in the world. Worldly men will say they know God, but they do not have any proof of it other than their words. Men in the world are more interested in gratifying the things of their flesh than their spirit. They might smoke a little weed, drink liquor, fornicate, listen to worldly (sexually explicit) music, and the like. The bad thing is, because these men may have gone to church as a child or know a few scriptures, it can become a challenge not to get entangled with them. You must discern early who sent this person into your life, God or Satan.

There was a season in my life where I was always getting hit on by thugs. I mean gold teeth, pants sagging, no job...a nightmare. I once met a man at the grocery store while I was on vacation from work. He asked me what I was doing off, and I told him I was on vacation. He said he was on vacation from work too. He even told me the name of the company and his job title. The thing was, I eventually went back to

121

DANIELLE WILIAMS

work, and after a few weeks of conversing with him, I realized he did not have a legal job at all. I am so happy that season of my life is over.

Those that are not in our same lane are not equally yoked with us; and dating someone who is not in your same lane will cause conflict. They will lead us down a dark path because, in the matter of relationships, the man is the head, and we are to follow him. If you follow this man who is not in love with God, where will this put you?

When we are in relationships with those who are not in our same lane, we spend endless hours trying to evangelize them to change their lifestyle. We will pray and pray to God to touch them. We will invite them to church and go on fast with us, all to no avail. In this person's heart, there is no desire to go after God the way you do. In some instances, they will go to church with you just to get closer to you. In John 6:44, the Bible says, *"No one can come to me unless the Father who sent me draws them, and I will raise them up at the last day."* The person you are dating must be drawn by God.

What should you do in this instance where you have fallen for a person you are not in the same lane with? Pray for them, but do not be yoked to them. Give them space they need to allow God to work on their heart. Trust God and have faith that if this relationship is of God, it will work out for your good. Understand the differences

122

between your beliefs and be open to God showing you His will in this relationship. If God reveals to you that this relationship is not of Him, you must let it go. We women of God cannot help the person we attract, but we can keep ourselves from entertaining and falling in love with the wrong one.

BREAKING UP

When you come to the realization that you are involved with the wrong individual and begin to feel you have made a poor decision and that you need a way out, first approach the man you are dating and let him know that you need your space; and that it is nothing he did, but it is you. Tell him you need time to focus on the things of God and better yourself, and you will not be able to concentrate on the relationship with him as needed. If that does not work, just tell him repeatedly that he is not the one for you. Be creative; you know this individual, so you should have an idea of how to get out of the relationship. The sooner, the better and do not be over dramatic and please, consider their feelings. Matthew 12:36 says that *"every idle word that men speak, they shall give account thereof in the day of judgment."* Do not allow this person to linger in your life. It is important to close the door and leave it closed.

THE LONELINESS

Being single in God can be a very lonely place. The closer you get to God, the less you seem to have things in common with other people. At this time, you must keep yourself busy with your purpose in God. God has given you a purpose and specific assignments that you need to get busy on. Begin to pray to God for revelation on what you should be doing at this time, the part of God's plan for your life. Focus less on dating and finding the right person and focus more on the things of God and pleasing Him. God will make His plan and purpose known as you seek Him with your whole heart.

This is a great time to build your intimacy level with God. It is an insult to ignore His presence. It is perfectly fine to sit and have a full conversation with God, let Him know what is going on in your life. Tell Him all of your cares because He cares for you. Ask Him the questions you may have and wait for a response. God loves you and will respond to you. His desire is to direct your life, so talking to Him and listening to Him will allow you to receive those plans.

When you are in need of companionship, find a younger cousin or relative you can spend time with, maybe even a neighbor's child who may need mentorship. There is always a younger child who would enjoy spending quality time with you.

You may even opt for something simple like, going out for ice cream or a snowball, catching a movie, or going bowling. Do not fill this companionship gap with the opposite sex. It will put you in a bad predicament. Investing positive energy in others at this time is a good way to encourage yourself and please the Lord.

GET YOUR JOY BACK

"*These things I have spoken to you, that my joy may remain in you and that your joy may be full*" John 15:11. Having joy is a key ingredient to having happiness. To increase in joy, you must take on positive traits like peace, thankfulness, understanding, and patience. To contain joy, we must reject feelings of depression and self-pity.

When you are feeling down or depressed and missing the person you were led by God to cut off, you must LET IT GO and ask God to restore His joy back inside you. The very last thing you want to do is being disobedient to God. God will show you signs if this is the person He has destined to be in your life. If it is not, let go immediately and deal with the feelings you may still have for him.

A lot of us are sad after a relationship ends because we really liked the person and may have fallen in love with them. I am so sorry if this is how you feel; I truly understand, but being in God's perfect will should be our #1 goal. After the person has left, you may cry at times, walk around moping, and may even have to ask yourself, what is wrong with me? What is wrong is that you need to change your perspective on this relationship and line your mind up with the will of God for your life.

If God said this is not the relationship for you, then it is not. Now receive the joy of the Lord. The Bible says in the book of Nehemiah Chapter 8 that the joy of the Lord is your strength. You may ask the question, what reason do I have to be happy or have joy when I am single and unhappy? Paul said in the book of Acts Chapter 26:2 that he *thinks* himself happy. Having joy is all about shifting our thoughts towards God. You are alive; you have your strength; you are a child of God; you are beautiful; God loves you; you have your health and a sound mind. Allow God to fill you with His joy and know that you are on your way to perfection with God. The Bible says in Psalm 16:11, *"You make known to me the path of life; you will fill me with joy in your presence, with eternal pleasures at your right hand."*

When you seek the will of God for your life, and God makes that known to you, you will have pure joy. Knowing the purpose, will, and plan of God for your life will surely give you joy. If you think about the person you had to release in the relationship, you know in your heart of hearts that he was not from God and was not for you. There is something more that you desire in a relationship, and there is more that God has for you in a significant other; you must be patient and obedient to the Spirit of God to receive what He has for you. Allow God to fill you with His Holy Spirit, and you will receive joy. To enter into God's presence, you must be on one accord with Him, having let go of every relationship and thing that displeases Him.

In closing, I hope that after reading this book you have gained insight and clarity on dating for believers. We are not to carry on the way the world does, and we are always to seek the face of God. Dating should not be about what we see with our eyes, but what we see by the Spirit of God. In the book of Samuel 16:7, God says, "*Do not consider his appearance or his height, for I have rejected him. The Lord does not look at the things people look at. People look at the outward appearance, but the Lord looks at the heart.*" We are to have faith and trust that God knows you and has something very special in store for you. Trust God's plan for your life. Amen!

SCRIPTURES FOR ENCOURAGEMENT:

1. Isaiah 40:31 — Those that wait on God shall renew their strength, they shall mount up with wings like eagles; they shall run and not be weary, and they shall walk and not faint
2. James 4:7 — Submit yourselves, then to God. Resist the devil, and he will flee from you
3. Philippians 4:8 — Finally, brothers and sisters, whatever is true, whatever is noble, whatever is right, whatever is pure, whatever is lovely, whatever is admirable-if anything is excellent or praiseworthy-think about such things.
4. Hebrews 11:1 — Now faith is the substance of things hoped for, the evidence of things not seen.
5. Psalm 37: 3-4 — Trust in the Lord and do good; dwell in the land and enjoy safe pasture. Take delight in the Lord, and he will give you the desires of your heart.
6. Hebrews 4:15 — For we do not have a high priest who is unable to sympathize with our weakness, but one who in every respect has been tempted as we are, yet without sin.
7. Philippians 4:11 — No matter what state we find ourselves in, married or single, we

are to be content.

8. Jeremiah 29:11 — I alone know the plans I have for you, plans to bring you prosperity and not disaster, plans to bring about the future you hope for.

9. Isaiah 54:5 — The Lord All-Powerful, the Holy God of Israel, rules all the earth. He is your Creator and husband, and he will rescue you.

10. Psalm 3:3 — But thou, O Lord, art a shield for me; my glory, and the lifter up of mine head.

www.ingramcontent.com/pod-product-compliance
Lightning Source LLC
Chambersburg PA
CBHW031625040426
42452CB00007B/675

* 9 7 8 0 9 9 7 7 1 4 1 1 1 *